KNIT MODERN SCANDI SWEATERS

MARITA CLEMENTZ

KNITTING PATTERNS FOR BRIGHT AND BEAUTIFUL NORDIC KNITS

DAVID & CHARLES
— PUBLISHING —

www.davidandcharles.com

KNIT MODERN SCANDI SWEATERS

MARITA CLEMENTZ

CONTENTS

Projects

INTRODUCTION

I was born on the west coast of Sweden, between the mountains and the sea, and I have always loved being out and about in nature, spending time in beautiful surroundings.

I have been creative for as long as I can remember. Since I was a little girl, I have sewed and designed clothes for myself (and others, including my dolls!), crocheted, woven, made bobbin lace and knitted. I have always taken great pleasure in colour and shape. Designing my own patterns and working with different colours brings me so much joy and satisfaction.

Some years ago, I started knitting a lot of Icelandic sweaters and discovered that I love yarn made from wool and natural fibres. I also love hiking, so wool sweaters are perfect for that side of my life!

Gradually, I began to want to use more colours and patterns – to go all out and be bold. I soon realised that there were few knitting patterns out there that dared to break with tradition, so I started creating my own patterns and trying out new colour combinations, which was so much fun.

Nature is a great source of inspiration for me – colourful flowers, the mountainous Scandinavian landscape, a sunset, an apple hanging from its tree – ideas for colour and shape can be found everywhere. My head is full of ideas for new patterns and ways to use colour; inspiration comes to me all the time and I hardly have to time to bring all my ideas to life.

There is a lot of work behind every single design in these pages, and each one represents countless hours of knitting, and pondering over colours and yarn choices. I am very proud and happy to share my designs with you. I hope you like the garments and are inspired to make them, and that you enjoy experimenting with different colours.

Happy Knitting!

Marita Clementz

TOOLS & MATERIALS

As well as the different yarns you will use, there are a few tools that you will need to make the patterns in this book. It's a good idea to have all your useful craft tools in one place so that you can have them to hand when you need them.

KNITTING NEEDLES

For sweaters knitted in DK (light worsted) weight yarn I have used 3.5mm (US size 4) circular needles for the main body. For sweaters knitted in aran (worsted) weight yarn I have used 4.5mm (US size 7) circular needles for the main body. For the rib sections I used smaller needles: 3mm (US size 3) for aran yarn and 3.5mm (US size 4) for DK yarn.

Circular needles

I prefer steel circular needles but you can use bamboo, wood or plastic if you prefer. You will need different cable lengths for different parts of the sweater, as noted in the pattern. Interchangeable circular needles are useful when you need to change needle sizes or cable lengths.

Double-pointed needles (DPNs)

I use double-pointed wood needles for the rib at the end of the sleeves. Wood or bamboo needles are good because they don't slip out of the stitches very easily, so the stitches stay in place.

OTHER USEFUL TOOLS

Stitch markers

I recommend locking or removable stitch markers in different colours to avoid confusion; I use green, yellow and pink ones. I always use green for the start of a round, yellow to mark the 'seams' and pink to mark the centre of each piece of work.

Measuring tape

It's best to use a fabric tape, but make sure it has not stretched with age.

Darning needle

I recommend using a needle with a blunt end to avoid splitting the yarn, and a large eye for ease of threading.

Scissors

You only need small scissors for snipping yarn.

Stitch holders or pieces of smooth waste yarn

You will need these for holding stitches that are not being worked on.

YARN

The yarns that I have used in this book are untreated (non-superwash) wool yarns that come from Scandinavia and Iceland.

The DK (light worsted) weight yarns are Filcolana Saga from Denmark, Hillesvåg Sol and Tinde from Norway, Novita Nalle from Finland, Rauma Finull from Norway and Järbo 2-tr Ull from Sweden. When knitted using 3.5mm (US size 4) needles they give a tension (gauge) of 22 sts and 30 rows to 10cm (4in).

The aran (worsted) weight yarns are Filcolana Peruvian from Denmark, Istex Plötulopi (pencil roving) and Léttlopi from Iceland, Novita Icelandic Wool and 7 Brothers from Finland, Hillesvåg Vidde, Varde and Luna from Norway, Rauma Fivel from Norway, and Järbo Svensk Ull 3-tr and Färgkraft Luxus Plus from Sweden. When knitted using 4.5mm (US size 7) needles they give a tension (gauge) of 18 sts and 24 rows to 10cm (4in).

See the Suppliers list at the end of this book to find the websites for the yarns used, or use the hashtag on each garment to search on Instagram for more colour and yarn inspiration.

It's not necessary to use untreated wool yarns – you can use any yarn of the same weight category as in the pattern. However, I recommend making a tension (gauge) swatch in the new yarn to ensure you achieve the tension specified in the project.

YARN CARE

Wool always becomes softer after washing and use. To wash one of these sweaters, place it in a bucket of warm water at a maximum temperature of 30°C (86°F) and leave it there until it is fully soaked, and no more air bubbles escape. You can also wash it the washing machine, using the cold wool cycle if it is available.

Dry the sweater flat and stretch it gently into shape. It is very important that you do not hang a wet sweater to dry, because this will cause it to stretch.

BEFORE YOU BEGIN

I have used Scandinavian and Icelandic wool yarns in creative and colourful ways in the patterns in this book because I am passionate about big, bright motifs. In the following pages you will find patterns for twelve unique raglan sweaters in two different yarn weights and a variety of colours.

YARN WEIGHTS

For some of the designs I have used DK (light worsted) weight yarns, and in others I have used aran (worsted) weight yarns. Two designs (Nordkap and Toini) have patterns in both yarn weights, so you can choose which one suits you. Each project also shows the level of difficulty – the larger and sparser the motifs in the sweater, the more difficult it will be to knit.

The pattern instructions give the yarn colours used for the sweater in the main picture. The colour combinations seen in additional photographs are listed in the Alternative Colourway box for each pattern.

CALCULATING INCREASES AND DECREASES

To calculate even spacing of increases and decreases, you need to know three numbers: the stitches on your needles; the increases/decreases to be made; and the stitches each increase/decrease is worked over.

Divide your total stitches by the number of increases (or decreases) you need to make, and that will tell you how many stitches each increase/decrease needs to be worked over.

For example, increasing from 92 to 100 stitches (8 stitches increased). 92 ÷ 8 = 11.5. Each increase needs to use up either 11 or 12 stitches, including the stitch you use for the increase, i.e., either (M1R, K10) or (M1R, K11). In this case, you'd work (M1R, K10) 4 times and (M1R, K11) 4 times.

For decreases, let's say you need to reduce your stitches from 62 to 48 (14 stitches decreased). 62 ÷ 14 = 4.5. Each decrease needs to use up either 4 or 5 stitches, including the 2 used in the decrease, i.e. either (k2, k2tog) or (k3, k2tog). In this case, you'd work (k2, k2tog) 8 times and (k3, k2tog) 6 times.

COLOUR DOMINANCE

When you knit patterns with two colours, which colour you allow to be dominant will make a big difference to the end result. Depending on how you hold the yarn, one of the colours will stand out more clearly than the other; this is the dominant colour.

If you hold both colours over the index finger of your left hand, the colour closest to the knitting (to the left and underneath the other yarn) will be dominant. If you hold one yarn in each hand, the yarn on the left will be dominant. I always make the motif colours dominant.

TOP: WHITE IS THE DOMINANT COLOUR

BOTTOM: PINK IS THE DOMINANT COLOUR

SIZES AND EASE

When choosing your size, think about how much space (ease) you want to have between your body and the sweater. Some of the sweaters pictured are worn with a small amount of ease (measured at the full chest), and some with more generous sizing. The measurements given in each pattern show the actual size of the garments, and do not include ease.

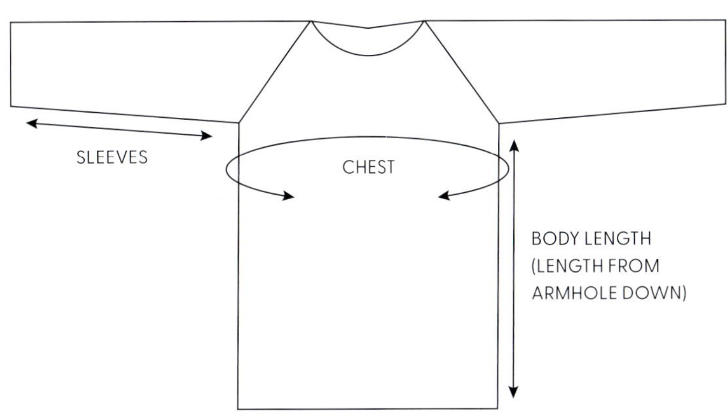

Taking measurements

Be careful not to pull the tape measure too tightly when measuring.

Chest circumference: Measured around the widest part of the chest.

Sleeve length: Measured from the armpit to the point at the wrist where you want the sleeve to end.

Body length: Measured from the underarm to the hem.

TENSION (GAUGE)

Always check your tension (gauge) by knitting a swatch at least 15 x 15cm (6 x 6in) so that you can count the stitches over 10cm (4in) easily. If you are making a colourwork design that is knitted in the round, the swatch should also be knitted in the round, using the same design. Making a swatch in one colour will not give you an accurate result, because people often knit more tightly when knitting motifs. If you get more or fewer stitches to 10cm (4in) than stated in the instructions, go up or down a needle size.

For my swatches, I usually cast on 25 sts to 4.5mm (US size 7) needles when using aran (worsted) or 30 sts onto 3.5mm (US size 4) needles when using DK (light worsted). I knit about 10cm (4in), then cast (bind) off, block it and then measure it.

Tip

You probably already have a favourite sweater that fits you perfectly. Measure the chest width, sleeve length and length from armholes to hem. Use these measurements to choose which size to make.

CONSTRUCTION

All the sweaters are knitted from top to bottom. A big advantage of knitting a sweater in this way is that you can check and adjust the length of the body and sleeves very easily by trying on the sweater from time to time before it's completely finished.

Seam markers

When you knit a sweater from the top down on circular needles, the sleeves and body are knitted at the same time once the neckband is complete. Between each of the four pieces – two sleeves, the back and the front – there are two stitches that are always knitted with the main colour to form a visual 'seam'. These seam stitches are not included when calculating the centre pattern stitch. The green and yellow markers in the photograph below show where these four seams are located. The green markers also indicate the start and end of the round.

Motif markers

The motifs are not worked continuously around the body, but are centralised on each section (front, back, and each sleeve), and separated by the seam stitches. It is important to place a marker on the centre stitch of each section (the pink markers in the photograph) so that the motif will be placed properly. You will need to count backwards from the centre stitch on the chart to identify which stitch to start on after the seam stitches have been worked. The centre of the motif is marked at the bottom of each chart (see also How To Read A Chart).

When working the main body, each size will start and end on a different chart stitch. To create a natural break in the pattern, when I cast on stitches under the sleeve I usually make sure the centre underarm stitch is knitted with the main colour again to create visual 'seams' on each side of the body, between the back and front pieces. Remember to place an additional stitch marker where this seam is positioned.

Tip

When working the raglan increases, mirror them on each side of the seams by working a left-leaning increase on one side, and a right-leaning one on the other. See General Techniques: Increase and Decrease.

NECKLINE

Six of the sweaters in this book – Birgitta, Lucky Garden, Nordkap Winter and Summer, Svalbard and Toini Summer – are knitted with short rows at the back neck, which makes the sweater sit a little higher on the back shoulders. However, all the sweaters can be knitted this way, so you can choose whether you want short rows or not. See General Techniques: German Short Rows for more details on working the stitches, and shape the neck as follows:

Neckline with short rows

1. Cut the yarn once you have worked the neckband, and rejoin it with right side facing you 2 sts before seam no. 4.
2. Working raglan increases on each side of every seam, knit until 2 sts after the second seam 3 marker. Turn.
3. Make a double stitch (DS), and purl to 4 sts after the second seam 4 marker, purling the 2 legs of the DS as 1 st. Turn.
4. Working raglan increases on each side of every seam, knit until 4 sts after the second seam 3 marker, knitting the 2 legs of the DS as 1 st. Turn.
5. Make a double stitch (DS), and purl to 6 sts after the second seam 4 marker, purling the 2 legs of the DS as 1 st. Cut the yarn, and rejoin yarn to seam 1.

Tip

I always work the short row neckline in the main colour, which means that there are no motifs in this area. To continue motifs up to the neck, I embroider duplicate stitches after finishing the sweater (see General Techniques: Duplicate Stitch).

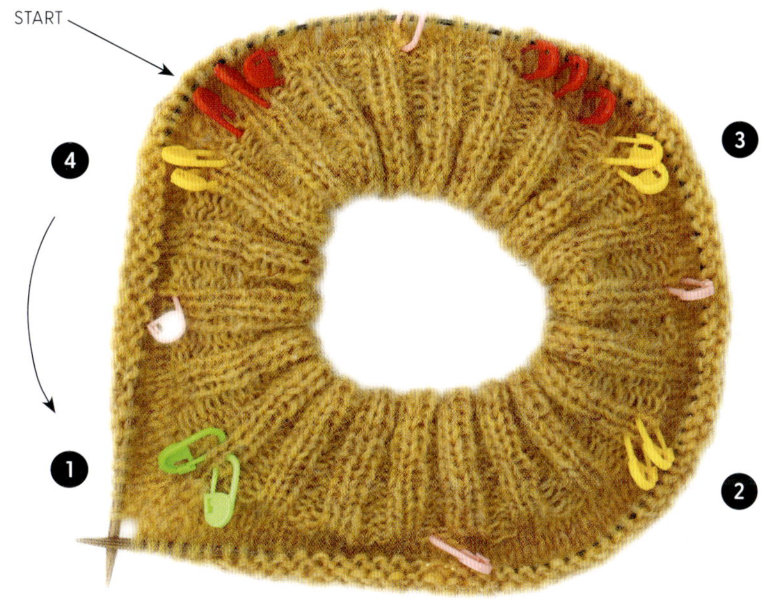

HOW TO READ A CHART

You'll start reading the chart in the lower right corner and read each round from right to left. Each square represents one stitch. Most of the charts show only one repeat of the pattern, or are marked to show the repeat section. Each chart shows the centre stitch of the repeat.

Different sizes and raglan increases

The patterns are all for raglan sweaters with repeating motifs, and each sweater has seven sizes. To make sure that the motif is centred correctly, the centre stitch of the chart must be worked on the centre stitch of each section (front, back, and each sleeve), on which you will have placed a marker (see Construction: Motif Markers).

To work out where to begin the chart for each section, you need to know how many stitches there are on each side of the central stitch. To find this out, subtract 1 (the central stitch) from the number of stitches in the section, then halve the answer. For example, 27 front stitches results in one central stitch with 13 stitches on each side (27 minus 1 is 26, half of 26 is 13).

Looking at the chart, count 13 stitches backwards from the marked central motif stitch to chart stitch 1 and then continue counting backwards from the last chart stitch. For example, the top chart to the right has 24 stitches, with stitch 12 as the marked central stitch. Counting backwards from 11 to 1, and then continuing from 24 means that the starting stitch in this case is 23.

Each time you make a raglan increase, you will have an extra stitch to work on each side of the chart, so again you will need to count backwards from the marked centre stitch to work out what colour the new stitch should be. This is to make sure that the pattern stays correct during the increases. Once you worked a few rows, you will have established the pattern, and it will be easy to see which stitch to work next. It might help you to make a few copies of the chart and tape them together into a long strip.

Adjusting the chart

You can choose to reposition the centre of the chart to place the motifs differently – for instance, the bottom chart to the right places the centre stitch in the middle of the flower. This will give a central flower at the neckline. If the centre stitch is moved to between two flowers (the top right chart), there will be a flower on each side of the neckline instead. If you do this, to avoid confusion as you continue working I suggest you copy the chart and renumber it!

Note that some of the charts have a different centre point for the body and the sleeves – this is noted on each relevant chart.

Tip

The charts show the colours worked in the main project, but you can experiment with colours for a unique sweater! Knit with one contrast colour per row, but try adding more colours afterwards using duplicate stitch.

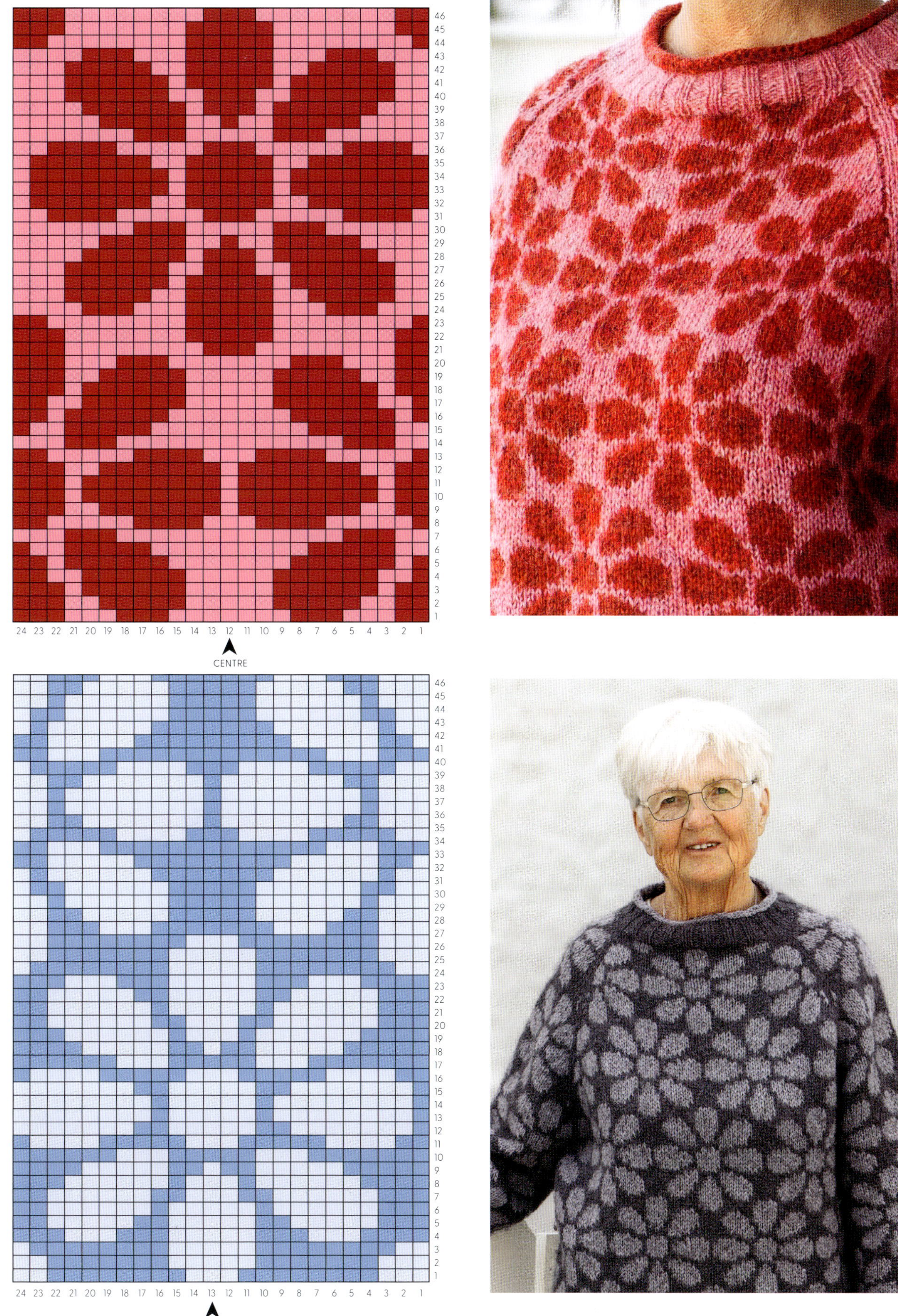
46 45 44 43 42 41 40 39 38 37 36 35 34 33 32 31 30 29 28 27 26 25 24 23 22 21 20 19 18 17 16 15 14 13 12 11 10 9 8 7 6 5 4 3 2 1
24 23 22 21 20 19 18 17 16 15 14 13 12 11 10 9 8 7 6 5 4 3 2 1
CENTRE
46 45 44 43 42 41 40 39 38 37 36 35 34 33 32 31 30 29 28 27 26 25 24 23 22 21 20 19 18 17 16 15 14 13 12 11 10 9 8 7 6 5 4 3 2 1
24 23 22 21 20 19 18 17 16 15 14 13 12 11 10 9 8 7 6 5 4 3 2 1
CENTRE

PROJECTS

ANEMONE *Sweater*

This was the first sweater I designed myself! Looking back, it was natural that it featured a floral motif. I love being out in my garden and in the forest, enjoying the shapes and colours of the flowers. To sit and knit surrounded by flowers is one of the best things I know.

#anemonesweater

SIZES

1 (2) 3 (4) 5 (6) 7

FINISHED GARMENT MEASUREMENTS

Sleeves:	48cm (19in) or desired length
Chest circumference:	85 (89) 97 (106) 115 (124) 133cm 34 (35½) 38½ (42½) 46 (49½) 53in
Body length:	44cm (17¼in) or desired length from underarm

TENSION (GAUGE)

18 stitches and 24 rows using 4.5mm (US size 7) needles = 10 x 10cm (4 x 4in)

YARN

Aran (worsted) weight yarn

Colours used for this sweater:

Main colour (MC)
Istex Plötulopi – Sunset Rose 1425
Contrast colour (CC)
Istex Plötulopi – Carmine Red 1430

AMOUNT OF YARN

Main colour (MC):	250 (300) 350 (350) 400 (450) 500g 8¾ (10½) 12¼ (12¼) 14 (16) 17¾oz
Contrast colour (CC):	200 (300) 300 (300) 350 (400) 450g 7 (10½) 10½ (10½) 12¼ (14) 16oz

KNITTING NEEDLES

Double-pointed needles:	3.5mm (US size 4)
Circular needles:	3.5mm (US size 4) and 4.5mm (US size 7), 40cm (16in)
Circular needles:	4.5mm (US size 7), 60cm (24in)
Circular needles:	3.5mm (US size 4) and 4.5mm (US size 7), 80cm (32in)

YOKE

Using CC and 3.5mm (US 4), 40cm (16in) circular needles, cast on 84 (84) 84 (92) 92 (92) 92 sts. Work St St for 5 rounds.

Change to MC and work 1 round of St St, then work in rib (k2, p2) for 4cm (1½in).

Change to 4.5mm (US 7), 60cm (24in) circular needles and work 1 round of St St, at the same time increasing by 8 (8) 8 (16) 16 (16) 16 sts distributing the increases evenly around.

Place markers according to the table below (see Before You Begin: Construction – Seam Markers). Place green markers over the first 2 sts (seam 1), and then place yellow markers over the 2 sts between each section (seams 2, 3 and 4). Also place a marker on the centre st of each piece, to centre the motif (see Before You Begin: Construction – Motif Markers).

Size	Stitches between the markers (seam 1, back, seam 2, sleeve, seam 3, front, seam 4, sleeve):
1	2, 27, 2, 15, 2, 27, 2, 15 sts
2	2, 27, 2, 15, 2, 27, 2, 15 sts
3	2, 29, 2, 13, 2, 29, 2, 13 sts
4	2, 37, 2, 13, 2, 37, 2, 13 sts
5	2, 37, 2, 13, 2, 37, 2, 13 sts
6	2, 39, 2, 11, 2, 39, 2, 11 sts
7	2, 39, 2, 11, 2, 39, 2, 11 sts

Begin working from the chart, making sure it is centred correctly, and working the first Raglan increase round on Round 1 of the chart as follows:

Raglan increase round: *Using MC, k2 seam sts, sm, M1R using correct chart colour for new st, work chart to next marker, M1L using correct chart colour for new st; repeat from * another 3 times. (8 sts increased around).

Repeat the Raglan increase round every second round until you have 244 (260) 276 (300) 324 (348) 364 sts, ending with an increase round. You will need to change to the 80cm (32in) cable as your stitches increase.

Work 9 more rounds without increases.

You will now divide the piece and work the body and sleeves separately.

Place each set of sleeve stitches together with 1 st from the seam on each side onto waste yarn or a stitch holder. Keep the front and back stitches and 1 st from the seam on each side on the 4.5mm (US 7), 80cm (32in) circular needle.

BODY (FRONT AND BACK)

Continue working according to the chart, casting on 9 (9) 9 (9) 11 (11) 11 sts for each underarm and placing a marker on each side of the central underarm st. Work this st in MC on every round.

Continue until the body measures 40cm (15¾in) or desired length from the underarm.

Change to 3.5mm (US 4), 80cm (32in) circular needles. Using MC, work in rib (k2, p2) for 4cm (1½in), then work 1 round of St St.

Change to CC. Work 5 rounds of St St, and then cast (bind) off.

CHART

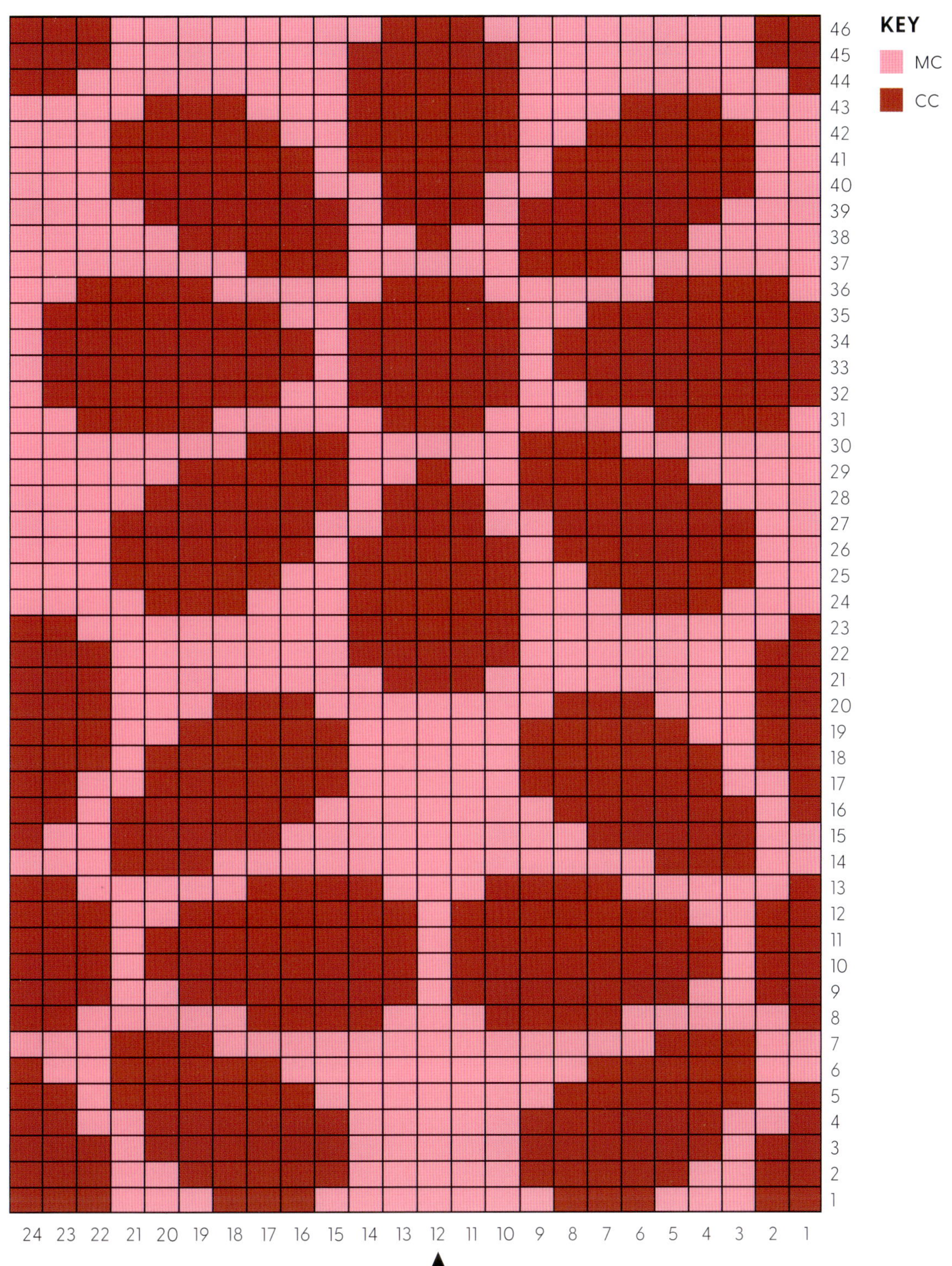

KEY

MC

CC

SLEEVES

Place one set of sleeve sts on 4.5mm (US 7), 40cm (16in) circular needles. Pick up 9 (9) 9 (9) 11 (11) 11 sts from the body sts you cast on for the underarm, and place a marker on each side of the centre underarm st. Work this st in MC on every round.

Continue working from the chart. After 8cm (3¼in), decrease 2 sts every 5 rounds (k2tog before the centre st, ssk after it) until 48 (48) 48 (56) 56 (56) 56 sts remain. Continue without decreasing until the sleeve measures 44cm (17¼in) or desired length.

Change to MC and work 1 round of St St, decreasing to 40 (40) 40 (44) 44 (44) 44 sts, distributing the decreases evenly around.

Change to 3.5m (US 4) DPNs and work in rib (k2, p2) for 4cm (1½in).

Change to CC and work 5 rounds of St St, then cast (bind) off. Work the other sleeve in the same way.

FINISHING

Weave in loose ends (see General Techniques: Finishing Techniques).

Place the sweater in a bucket of warm water (no more than 30°C (86°F)) and leave it until fully soaked. Dry flat and stretch into shape. Do not hang the sweater to dry, as this will make it stretch.

Tip

If you work right- and left-leaning decreases when shaping the sleeves (see General Techniques: Increase and Decrease) it will give your sleeves a neat, professional look.

Alternative Colourway

The colours I have used here are:

Main colour (MC)
Hillesvåg Varde – Greyish Lavender Blue 2128

Contrast colour (CC)
Hillesvåg Vidde – Lilac 338

Suggested other yarns:

Istex Léttlopi, Rauma Fivel, Novita Icelandic Wool, Novita 7 Brothers or other aran (worsted) weight yarn. Be sure to check the tension (gauge).

BIRGITTA
Sweater

I'm often told that my designs are bold, colourful and fun, and I like that people appreciate them. In this sweater, I wanted to use a large pattern to capture the clear Scandinavian light. This design is named after my mother.

#birgittasweater

SIZES

1 (2) 3 (4) 5 (6) 7

FINISHED GARMENT MEASUREMENTS

Sleeves:	46cm (18in) or desired length
Chest circumference:	85 (89) 97 (106) 115 (124) 133cm 34 (35½) 38½ (42½) 46 (49½) 53in
Body length:	40cm (15¾in) or desired length from underarm

TENSION (GAUGE)

18 stitches and 24 rows using 4.5mm (US size 7) needles = 10 x 10cm (4 x 4in)

YARN

Aran (worsted) weight yarn

Colours used for this sweater:

Main colour (MC)

Istex Léttlopi – Straw 1418

Contrast colours (CC)

1. Hillesvåg Luna – Coral 427
2. Hillesvåg Vidde – Orange 335
3. Novita Icelandic Wool – Peony 550
4. Hillesvåg Luna – Orange 422

AMOUNT OF YARN

Main colour (MC):	450 (500) 550 (600) 650 (700) 750g 16 (17¾) 19½ (21¼) 23 (24¾) 26½oz
Contrast colour (CC):	70 (80) 80 (90) 90 (90) 100g each colour 2½ (2¾) 2¾ (3¼) 3¼ (3¼) 3½oz each colour

KNITTING NEEDLES

Double pointed needles:	3.5mm (US size 4)
Circular needles:	3.5mm (US size 4) and 4.5mm (US size 7), 40cm (16in)
Circular needles:	4.5mm (US size 7), 60cm (24in)
Circular needles:	3.5mm (US size 4) and 4.5mm (US size 7), 80cm (32in)

YOKE

Using MC and 3.5mm (US 4), 40cm (16in) circular needles, cast on 88 (88) 88 (96) 96 (100) 100 sts. Work in rib (k2, p2) for 8cm (3¼in).

Change to 4.5mm (US 7), 60cm (24in) circular needles. Work 1 round of St St, at the same time increasing 4 (4) 4 (12) 12 (8) 8 sts distributing the increases evenly around. Cut the yarn, ready to work the short-row neck shaping on the back.

Place markers according to the table below (see Before You Begin: Construction – Seam Markers). Place a green marker on each side of the first 2 sts (seam 1), and a yellow marker on each side of the 2 sts for seams 2, 3 and 4.

Size	Stitches between the markers: (seam 1, back, seam 2, sleeve, seam 3, front, seam 4, sleeve)
1	2, 27, 2, 15, 2, 27, 2, 15 sts
2	2, 27, 2, 15, 2, 27, 2, 15 sts
3	2, 29, 2, 13, 2, 29, 2, 13 sts
4	2, 37, 2, 13, 2, 37, 2, 13 sts
5	2, 37, 2, 13, 2, 37, 2, 13 sts
6	2, 39, 2, 11, 2, 39, 2, 11 sts
7	2, 39, 2, 11, 2, 39, 2, 11 sts

NECKLINE WITH SHORT ROWS AT THE NECK

With the right side facing you, rejoin yarn 2 sts before seam 4 and work German Short Rows as follows:

Short row 1: K2, M1R, *sm, k2, sm, M1L, knit to next marker, M1R; repeat from * 2 more times, sm, M1L, k2, turn. You will have worked around to 2 sts after the second seam 3 marker.

Short row 2: DS, purl to second seam 4 marker, sm, p4, turn.

Short row 3: DS, knit to second marker for seam 3, working raglan increases each side of seams as for Short row 1, sm, M1L, k4, turn.

Short row 4: DS, purl to second seam 4 marker, sm, p6. Cut the yarn.

Place a marker on the centre st of each section (see Before You Begin: Construction – Motif Markers).

With the right side facing you, rejoin MC to the first st of seam 1 (between the green markers). Begin working from the chart, making sure it is centred correctly, and working the first Raglan increase round on Round 1 of the chart as follows:

Raglan increase round: *Using MC, k2 seam sts, sm, M1R using correct chart colour for new st, work chart to next marker, M1L using correct chart colour for new st; repeat from * another 3 times. (8 sts increased around).

Repeat Raglan increase round every second round until you have 244 (260) 276 (300) 324 (348) 364 sts, ending with an increase round. You will need to change to the 80cm (32in) cable as your sts increase.

Continue in pattern for 9 more rounds, working raglan increases only on the sleeves every second round.

You will now divide the piece and work the body and sleeves separately.

Place each set of sleeve sts together with 1 st from the seam on each side onto waste yarn or a stitch holder. Keep the front and back sts and 1 st from the seam on each side on the 4.5mm (US 7), 80cm (32in) circular needle.

BODY (FRONT AND BACK)

Continue working from the chart, casting on 9 (9) 9 (9) 11 (11) 11 sts for each underarm and placing a marker either side of the central underarm st on each side. Work this st in MC on every round.

Continue until body measures 36cm (14¼in) or desired length from underarm.

Using MC only, work 1 round of St St.

Change to 3.5mm (US 4), 80cm (32in) circular needles. Work in rib (k2, p2) for 4cm (1½in), then cast (bind) off.

CHART

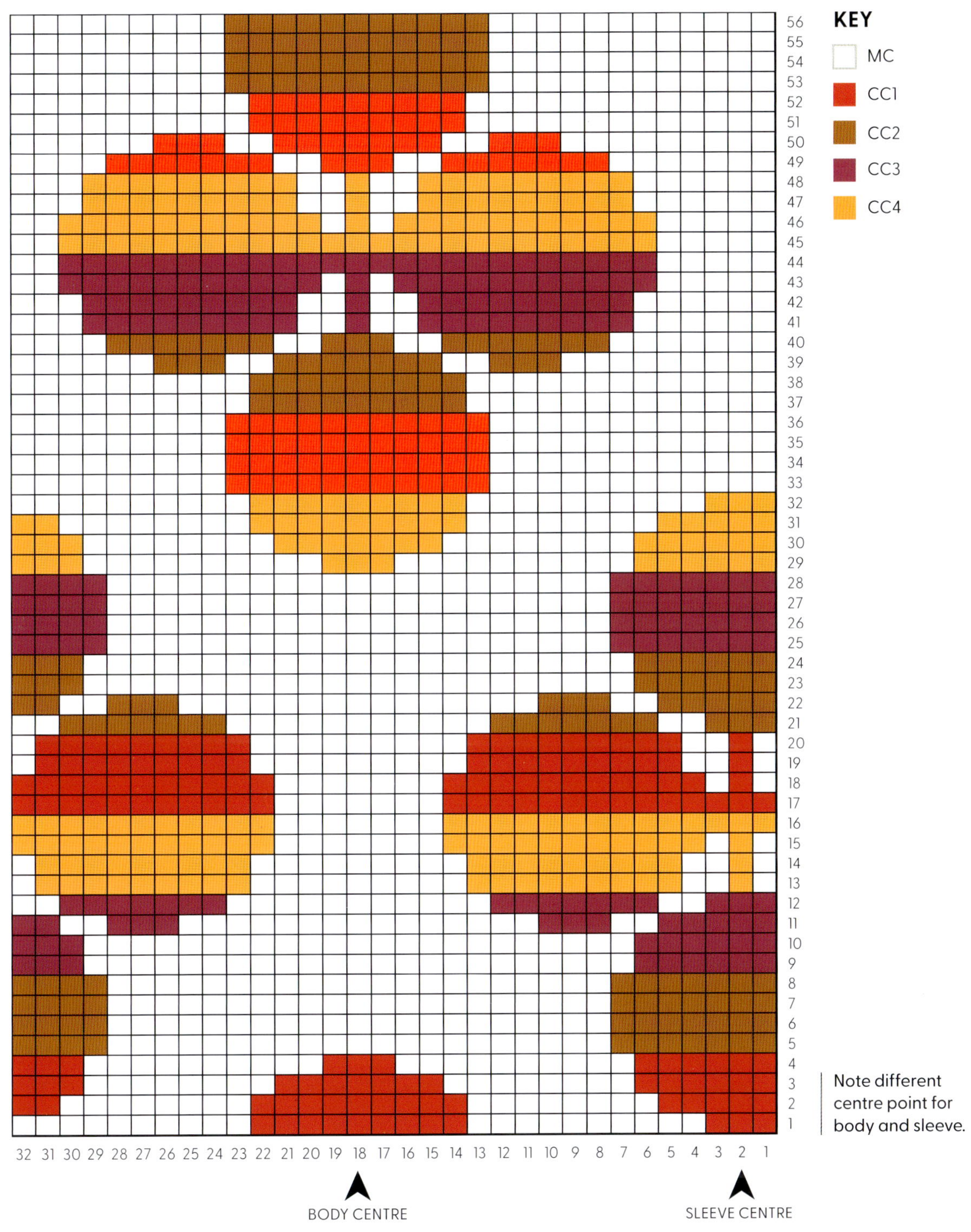

KEY

- MC
- CC1
- CC2
- CC3
- CC4

Note different centre point for body and sleeve.

SLEEVE

Place one set of sleeve sts on 4.5mm (US 7), 40cm (16in) circular needles. Pick up 9 (9) 9 (9) 11 (11) 11 sts from the body sts you cast on for the underarm, and place a marker on each side of the centre underarm st. Work this st in MC on every round.

Continue working from the chart until sleeve measures 42cm (16½in) or desired length.

Using MC only, work 1 round of St St, at the same time decreasing to 40 (40) 40 (44) 44 (44) 44 sts, evenly distributing the decreases around.

Change to 3.5mm (US4) DPNs. Work in rib (k2, p2) for 4cm (1½in), then cast (bind) off. Work the other sleeve in the same way.

FINISHING

Weave in loose ends. Turn the sweater inside out, and fold the neckband in half, with the right side facing you. Use whip stitch to sew the cast-on edge of the neckband loosely to the inside of the neck (see General Techniques: Finishing Techniques for weaving in ends and whip stitch instructions).

To continue the motifs up to the neck on the short row section, embroider the missing sections in duplicate stitch (see General Techniques: Duplicate Stitch) using the chart as a guide.

Place the sweater in a bucket of warm water (no more than 30°C (86°F)) and leave it until fully soaked. Dry flat and stretch into shape. Do not hang the sweater to dry, as this will make it stretch.

Tip

If you want the short-row section to feature the motif pattern, embroider it on after the sweater is finished, using duplicate stitch (see General Techniques: Colourwork)

Alternative Colourway

The colours I have used here are:

Main colour (MC)
Rauma Fivel – Natural 01

Contrast colour 1 (CC1)
Filcolana Peruvian – Rime Frost 281

Contrast colour 2 (CC2)
Filcolana Peruvian – Green Tea 355

Contrast colour 3 (CC3)
Rauma Fivel – Light Turquoise 23

Contrast colour 4 (CC4)
Filcolana Peruvian – Alaskan Blue 141

Suggested other yarns:

Hillesvåg Varde, Novita 7 Brothers/Hehku, Istex Léttlopi/Plötulopi, Novita Icelandic Wool, Järbo Svensk Ull 3-tr or other aran (worsted) weight yarn. Be sure to check the tension (gauge).

BOLLERINA

Sweater

Most of us played with balls when we were little (in Swedish, 'boll' means ball). I was inspired to be playful, mixing colours and using a ball-shaped motif. The colours can be varied endlessly, so let playfulness rule when looking for your own unique colour combinations.

#bollerinasweater

SIZES

1 (2) 3 (4) 5 (6) 7

FINISHED GARMENT MEASUREMENTS

Sleeves:	49cm (19¼in) or desired length
Chest circumference:	85 (89) 97 (106) 115 (124) 133cm 34 (35½) 38½ (42½) 46 (49½) 53in
Body length:	43cm (17in) or desired length from underarm

TENSION (GAUGE)

18 stitches and 24 rows using 4.5mm (US size 7) needles = 10 x 10cm (4 x 4in)

YARN

Aran (worsted) weight yarn

Colours used for this sweater:

Main colour (MC)
Istex Plötulopi – Amethyst 2026

Contrast colour 1 (CC1)

Istex Plötulopi – Sunset Rose 1425

Contrast colour 2 (CC2)
Istex Plötulopi – Golden Blush 2028

AMOUNT OF YARN

Main colour (MC):	200 (200) 200 (250) 300 (350) 400g 7 (7) 7 (8¾) 10½ (12¼) 14oz
Contrast colour 1 (CC1):	100 (100) 100 (150) 150 (200) 200g 3½ (3½) 3½ (5¼) 5¼ (7) 7oz
Contrast colour 2 (CC2):	100 (100) 100 (150) 150 (200) 200g 3½ (3½) 3½ (5¼) 5¼ (7) 7oz

KNITTING NEEDLES

Double pointed needles:	3.5mm (US size 4)
Circular needles:	3.5mm (US size 4) and 4.5mm (US size 7), 40cm (16in)
Circular needles:	4.5mm (US size 7), 60cm (24in)
Circular needles:	3.5mm (US size 4) and 4.5mm (US size 7), 80cm (32in)

YOKE

Using MC and 3.5mm (US 4), 40cm (16in) circular needles, cast on 88 (88) 88 (96) 96 (96) 96 sts. Work in rib (k2, p2) for 3.5cm (1¼in).

Change to 4.5mm (US 7), 60cm (24in) circular needles and work 1 round of St St, at the same time increasing 4 (4) 4 (12) 12 (12) 12 sts, distributing the increases evenly around.

Place markers according to the table below (see Before You Begin: Construction – Seam Markers). Place a green marker on each side of the first 2 sts (seam 1), and a yellow marker on each side of the 2 sts for seams 2, 3 and 4. Also place a marker on the centre st of each section to centre the motif (see Before You Begin: Construction – Motif Markers).

Size	Stitches between the markers: (seam 1, back, seam 2, sleeve, seam 3, front, seam 4, sleeve)
1	2, 27, 2, 15, 2, 27, 2, 15 sts
2	2, 27, 2, 15, 2, 27, 2, 15 sts
3	2, 29, 2, 13, 2, 29, 2, 13 sts
4	2, 37, 2, 13, 2, 37, 2, 13 sts
5	2, 37, 2, 13, 2, 37, 2, 13 sts
6	2, 39, 2, 11, 2, 39, 2, 11 sts
7	2, 39, 2, 11, 2, 39, 2, 11 sts

Begin working from the chart, making sure it is centred correctly, and working the first Raglan increase round on Round 1 of the chart as follows:

Raglan increase round: *Using MC, k2 seam sts, sm, M1R using correct chart colour for new st, work chart to next marker, M1L using correct chart colour for new st; repeat from * another 3 times. (8 sts increased around).

Repeat the Raglan increase round every second round until you have 244 (260) 276 (300) 324 (348) 364 sts, ending with an increase round. You will need to change to the 80cm (32in) cable as your sts increase.

Continue in pattern for 9 more rounds, working raglan increases only on the sleeves every second round.

You will now divide the piece and work the body and sleeves separately.

Place each set of sleeve sts together with 1 st from the seam on each side onto waste yarn or a stitch holder. Keep the front and back sts and 1 st from the seam on each side on the 4.5mm (US 7), 80cm (32in) circular needle.

BODY (FRONT AND BACK)

Continue working from the chart, casting on 9 (9) 9 (9) 11 (11) 11 sts for each underarm and placing a marker either side of the central underarm st on each side. Work this st in MC on every round.

Continue until the body measures 35cm (13¾in) or desired length from underarm.

Work 1 round of St St and then increase to 168 (176) 188 (212) 228 (244) 256 sts, evenly distributing the increases around.

Change to 3.5mm (US 4), 80cm (32in) circular needles. Work in rib (k2, p2) for 8cm (3¼in), and then cast (bind) off.

CHART

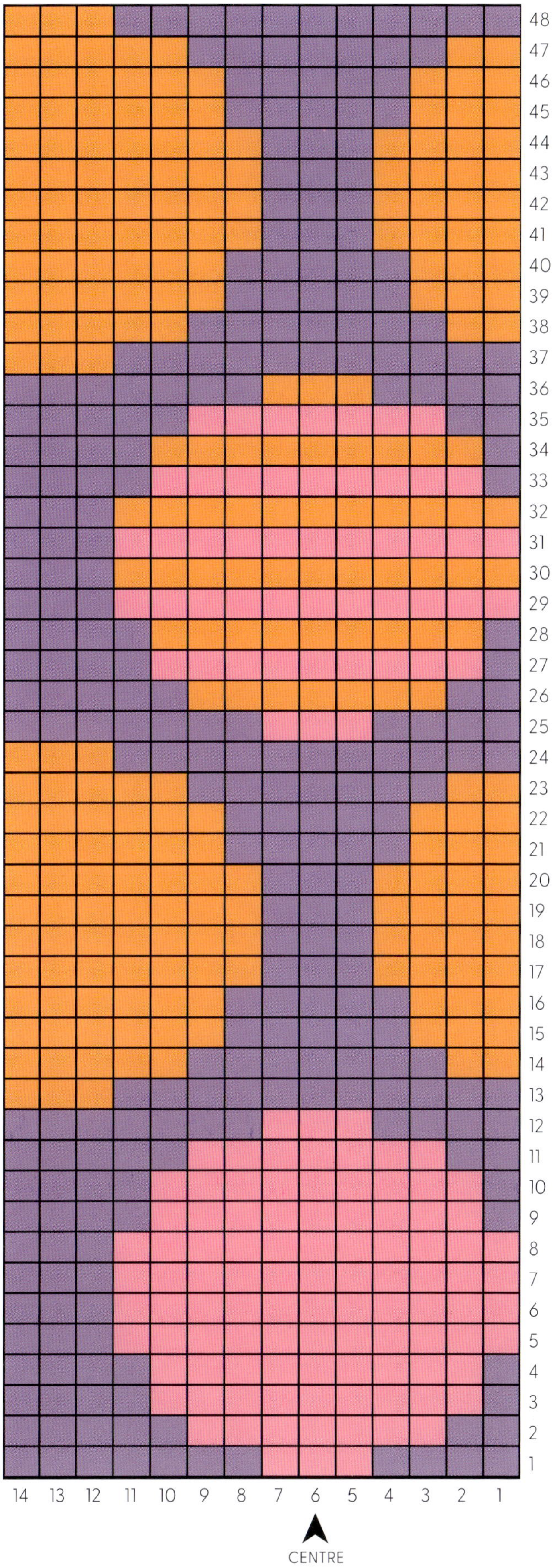

CENTRE

The contrast colours used in the Alternative Colourway run in this order:
CC1
CC2
CC3
CC4
CC1
CC5
CC2
CC3
CC4
CC6
CC1
CC5
CC3

SLEEVES

Place one set of sleeve sts on 4.5mm (US 7), 40cm (16in) circular needles. Pick up 9 (9) 9 (9) 11 (11) 11 sts from the body sts you cast on for the underarm, and place a marker on each side of the centre underarm st. Work this st in MC on every round.

Continue working from the chart until the sleeve measures 41cm (16¼in) or desired length.

Change to MC and work 1 round of St St, at the same time decreasing to 40 (40) 40 (44) 44 (44) 44 sts, evenly distributing the decreases around.

Change to 3.5mm (US 4) DPNs. Work in rib (k2, p2) for 8cm (3¼in), and then cast (bind) off. Work the other sleeve in the same way.

FINISHING

Weave in loose ends (see General Techniques: Finishing Techniques).

Place the sweater in a bucket of warm water (no more than 30°C (86°F)) and leave it until fully soaked. Dry flat and stretch into shape. Do not hang the sweater to dry, as this will make it stretch.

Tip

When you pick up the stitches for the sleeves, count them to see if you can work the whole pattern around. If you have one or two stitches too many or too few, you can decrease or increase stitches here to make the full pattern.

Alternative Colourway

The colours I have used here are:

Main colour (MC)
Istex Plötulopi – White 0001

Contrast colour 1 (CC1)
Istex Plötulopi – Light Grey 1027

Contrast colour 2 (CC2)
Istex Plötulopi – Light Blues Blue 2023

Contrast colour 3 (CC3)
Istex Plötulopi – Light Beige 0003

Contrast colour 4 (CC4)
Färgkraft Luxus Plus – Aqua Soft V

Contrast colour 5 (CC5)
Istex Plötulopi – Ash 1026

Contrast colour 6 (CC6)
Istex Plötulopi – Ivory Beige 1038

Suggested other yarns:

Istex Léttlopi, Fivel, Hillesvåg Vidde/Varde/Luna, Filcolana Peruvian, Novita 7 Brothers, Viking Alpe or other aran (worsted) weight yarn. Be sure to check the tension (gauge).

LOFOTEN
Sweater

Lofoten, in northern Scandinavia, is a place I've returned to several times. The scenery is spectacular, with high, jagged mountains rising out of the sea to meet the sky. I recommend that you visit this fantastic area, which provided the inspiration for this pattern.

#lofotensweater

SIZES

1 (2) 3 (4) 5 (6) 7

FINISHED GARMENT MEASUREMENTS

Sleeves:	50cm (19¾in) or desired length
Chest circumference:	85 (89) 97 (106) 115 (124) 133cm 34 (35½) 38½ (42½) 46 (49½) 53in
Body length:	48cm (19in) or desired length from underarm

TENSION (GAUGE)

18 stitches and 24 rows using 4.5mm (US size 7) needles = 10 x 10cm (4 x 4in)

YARN

Aran (worsted) weight yarn

Colours used for this sweater:

Main colour (MC)
Istex Plötulopi – Light Beige 0003

Contrast colours (CC):

1. Istex Plötulopi – Clover Green 1423
2. Istex Léttlopi – Spring Green 1406
3. Istex Plötulopi – Gulf Stream 2025
4. Istex Léttlopi – Glacier Blue 1404
5. Istex Léttlopi – Stone Blue 9418
6. Istex Léttlopi – Ocean Blue 9419
7. Istex Léttlopi – Lagoon 9423
8. Istex Léttlopi – Celery Green 9421

AMOUNT OF YARN

Main colour (MC):	250 (300) 350 (350) 400 (450) 500g 8¾ (10½) 12¼ (12¼) 14 (16) 17¾oz
Contrast colour (CC):	50g each colour 1¾oz each colour

KNITTING NEEDLES

Double pointed needles:	3.5mm (US size 4)
Circular needles:	3.5mm (US size 4) and 4.5mm (US size 7), 40cm (16in)
Circular needles:	4.5mm (US size 7), 60cm (24in)
Circular needles:	3.5mm (US size 4) and 4.5mm (US size 7), 80cm (32in)

YOKE

Using CC7 and 3.5mm (US 4), 40cm (16in) circular needles, cast on 84 (84) 84 (92) 92 (92) 92 sts. Work St St for 5 rounds.

Change to MC and work 1 round of St St.

Work in rib (k2, p2) for 4cm (1½in).

Change to 4.5mm (US 7), 60cm (24in) circular needles and work 1 round of St St, at the same time increasing 8 (8) 8 (16) 16 (16) 16 sts, distributing the increases evenly around.

Place markers according to the table below (see Before You Begin: Construction – Seam Markers).Place a green marker on each side of the first 2 sts (seam 1), and a yellow marker on each side of the 2 sts for seams 2, 3 and 4. Also place a marker on the centre st of each section to centre the motif (see Before You Begin: Construction – Motif Markers).

Size	Stitches between the markers: (seam 1, back, seam 2, sleeve, seam 3, front, seam 4, sleeve)
1	2, 27, 2, 15, 2, 27, 2, 15 sts
2	2, 27, 2, 15, 2, 27, 2, 15 sts
3	2, 29, 2, 13, 2, 29, 2, 13 sts
4	2, 37, 2, 13, 2, 37, 2, 13 sts
5	2, 37, 2, 13, 2, 37, 2, 13 sts
6	2, 39, 2, 11, 2, 39, 2, 11 sts
7	2, 39, 2, 11, 2, 39, 2, 11 sts

Begin working from the chart, making sure it is centred correctly, and working the first Raglan increase round on Round 1 of the chart as follows:

Raglan increase round: *Using MC, k2 seam sts, sm, M1R using correct chart colour for new st, work chart to next marker, M1L using correct chart colour for new st; repeat from * another 3 times. (8 sts increased around).

Repeat the first Raglan increase round every second round until you have 244 (260) 276 (300) 324 (348) 364 sts, ending with an increase round. You will need to change to the 80cm (32in) cable as your sts increase.

Work 9 more rounds without increases.

You will now divide the piece and work the body and sleeves separately.

Place each set of sleeve stitches together with 1 st from the seam on each side onto waste yarn or a stitch holder. Keep the front and back sts and 1 st from the seam on each side on the 4.5mm (US 7), 80cm (32in) circular needle.

BODY (FRONT AND BACK)

Continue working from the chart, casting on 9 (9) 9 (9) 11 (11) 11 sts for each underarm and placing a marker either side of the central underarm st on each side. Work this st in MC on every round.

Continue until the body measures 44cm (17¼in) or desired length from underarm.

Change to 3.5mm (US 4), 80cm (32in) circular needles. Using MC only, work in rib (k2, p2) for 4cm (1½in), then work 1 round of St St.

Change to CC7 and work 5 rounds of St St, then cast (bind) off.

CHART

KEY

- MC
- CC1
- CC2

Once you have worked Rows 1-20 using CCs 1 and 2, repeat these rows using CCs 3 and 4, then 5 and 6, and finally 7 and 8. Begin again using CCs 1 and 2 if you use all 8 CCs (or all 6 if you are making the Chocolate/Orange/Pink alternative colourway).

SLEEVES

Place one set of sleeve sts on 4.5mm (US 7), 40cm (16in) circular needles. Pick up 9 (9) 9 (9) 11 (11) 11 sts from the body sts you cast on for the underarm, and place a marker on each side of the centre underarm st. Work this st in MC on every round.

Continue working from the chart. After 8cm (3¼in), decrease 2 sts every 5 rounds (k2tog before the centre st, ssk after it) until 48 (48) 48 (56) 56 (56) 56 sts remain. Continue without decreasing until the sleeve measures 46cm (18in) or desired length from underarm.

Using MC only, work 1 round of St St, at the same time decreasing to 40 (40) 40 (44) 44 (44) 44 sts, evenly distributing the decreases around.

Change to 3.5mm (US 4) DPNs and work in rib (k2, p2) for 4cm (1½in).

Change to CC7 and work 5 rounds of St St then cast (bind) off. Work the other sleeve in the same way.

FINISHING

Weave in loose ends (see General Techniques: Finishing Techniques).

Place the sweater in a bucket of warm water (no more than 30°C (86°F)) and leave it until fully soaked. Dry flat and stretch into shape. Do not hang the sweater to dry, as this will make it stretch.

Alternative Colourways

Orange/pink

The colours I have used here are:

Main colour (MC)
Istex Plötulopi – White 0001

Contrast colour 1 (CC1)
Istex Plötulopi – Sunset Rose 1425

Contrast colour 2 (CC2)
Hillesvåg Luna – Orange 422

Chocolate/orange/pink

The colours I have used here are:

Main colour (MC)
Istex Plötulopi – Chocolate 1032

Contrast colour 1 (CC1)
Istex Plötulopi – Dark Amber 1426

Contrast colour 2 (CC2)
Hillesvåg Vidde – Orange 335

Contrast colour 3 (CC3)
Hillesvåg Varde – Pink 2110

Contrast colour 4 (CC4)
Hillesvåg Varde – Dusty Pink 2137

Contrast colour 5 (CC5)
Istex Plötulopi – Light Beige 0003

Contrast colour 6 (CC6)
Istex Plötulopi – Oatmeal 1030

Suggested other yarns:

Rauma Fivel, Novita Icelandic Wool, Hillesvåg Luna, Novita 7 Brothers or other aran (worsted) weight yarn. Be sure to check the tension (gauge).

LUCKY GARDEN *Sweater*

According to Western tradition, the four-leaf clover is a symbol of good luck, especially if found by chance. The quatrefoil (meaning 'four leaves') motif appears in the art and architecture of many cultures and religions. This pattern came to me quite naturally, and I knitted the sweater for my son to give him all the happiness I can.

#luckygardensweater

SIZES

1 (2) 3 (4) 5 (6) 7

FINISHED GARMENT MEASUREMENTS

Sleeves:	56cm (22in) or desired length
Chest circumference:	85 (89) 97 (106) 115 (124) 133cm 34 (35½) 38½ (42½) 46 (49½) 53in
Body length:	50cm (19¾in) or desired length from underarm

TENSION (GAUGE)

18 stitches and 24 rows using 4.5mm (US size 7) needles = 10 x 10cm (4 x 4in)

YARN

Aran (worsted) weight yarn

Colours used for this sweater:

Main colour (MC)
Istex Léttlopi – Ash 0054

Contrast colours (CC)

1. Istex Léttlopi – Spring Green 1406
2. Istex Léttlopi – Lyme Grass 1706
3. Istex Léttlopi – Celery Green 9421
4. Järbo Svensk Ull 3-tr – Northern Lights 59013
5. Istex Léttlopi – Lagoon 9423
6. Istex Plötulopi – Brown 0009
7. Istex Plötulopi – Chocolate 1032
8. Istex Léttlopi – Grape 9432

AMOUNT OF YARN

Main colour (MC):	350 (400) 400 (450) 500 (550) 600g 12¼ (14) 14 (16) 17¾ (19½) 21¼oz
Contrast colour 1 (CC1:)	50 (50) 50 (50) 50 (50) 100g 1¾ (1¾) 1¾ (1¾) 1¾ (1¾) 3½oz
Contrast colours 2, 3 (CC2, CC3):	50 (50) 50 (50) 50 (100) 100g each colour 1¾ (1¾) 1¾ (1¾) 1¾ (3½) 3½oz each colour
Contrast colours 4, 5, 8 (CC4, CC5, CC8):	50g each colour 1¾oz each colour
Contrast colours 6, 7 (CC6, CC7):	20 (20) 20 (20) 30 (30) 30g each colour ¾ (¾) ¾ (¾) 1 (1) 1oz each colour

KNITTING NEEDLES

Double pointed needles:	3.5mm (US size 4)
Circular needles:	3.5mm (US size 4) and 4.5mm (US size 7), 40cm (16in)
Circular needles:	4.5mm (US size 7), 60cm (24in)
Circular needles:	3.5mm (US size 4) and 4.5mm (US size 7), 80cm (32in)

YOKE

Using MC and 3.5mm (US 4), 40cm (16in) circular needles, cast on 88 (88) 88 (96) 96 (100) 100 sts. Work in rib (k2, p2) for 8cm (3¼in), or 18cm (7in) if you prefer a turtleneck.

Change to 4.5mm (US 7), 60cm (24in) circular needles and work 1 round of St St, at the same time increasing 4 (4) 4 (12) 12 (8) 8 sts, distributing the increases evenly around. Cut the yarn, ready to work the short-row neck shaping on the back.

Place markers according to the table below (see Before You Begin: Construction – Seam Markers). Place a green marker on each side of the first 2 sts (seam 1), and a yellow marker on each side of the 2 sts for seams 2, 3 and 4.

Size	Stitches between the markers: (seam 1, back, seam 2, sleeve, seam 3, front, seam 4, sleeve)
1	2, 27, 2, 15, 2, 27, 2, 15 sts
2	2, 27, 2, 15, 2, 27, 2, 15 sts
3	2, 29, 2, 13, 2, 29, 2, 13 sts
4	2, 37, 2, 13, 2, 37, 2, 13 sts
5	2, 37, 2, 13, 2, 37, 2, 13 sts
6	2, 39, 2, 11, 2, 39, 2, 11 sts
7	2, 39, 2, 11, 2, 39, 2, 11 sts

NECKLINE WITH SHORT ROWS AT THE NECK

With the right side facing you, rejoin yarn 2 sts before seam 4 and work German Short Rows as follows:

Short row 1: K2, M1R, *sm, k2, sm, M1L, knit to next marker, M1R; repeat from * 2 more times, sm, M1L, k2, turn. You will have worked around to 2 sts after the second seam 3 marker.

Short row 2: DS, purl to second seam 4 marker, sm, p4, turn.

Short row 3: DS, knit to second marker for seam 3, working raglan increases each side of seams as for Short row 1, sm, M1L, k4, turn.

Short row 4: DS, purl to second seam 4 marker, sm, p6. Cut the yarn.

Place a marker on the centre st of each piece to centre the motif (see Before You Begin: Construction – Motif Markers).

With the right side facing you, rejoin MC to the first st of seam 1 (between the green markers). Begin working from the chart starting with Round 3, making sure it is centred correctly, and working the first Raglan increase round on Round 3 of the chart as follows:

Raglan increase round: *Using MC, k2 seam sts, sm, M1R using correct chart colour for new st, work chart to next marker, M1L using correct chart colour for new st; repeat from * another 3 times. (8 sts increased).

Repeat the Raglan increase round every second round until you have 244 (260) 276 (300) 324 (348) 364 sts, ending with an increase round. You will need to change to the 80cm (32in) cable as your sts increase.

Continue in pattern for 9 more rounds, working raglan increases only on the sleeves every second round (8 sts increased for each sleeve).

You will now divide the piece and work the body and sleeves separately.

Place each set of sleeve stitches together with 1 st from the seam on each side onto waste yarn or a stitch holder. Keep the front and back sts and 1 st from the seam on each side on the 4.5mm (US 7), 80cm (32in) circular needle.

BODY (FRONT AND BACK)

Work the body according to the chart, adding 9 (9) 9 (9) 11 (11) 11 sts for each underarm. Work until the body measures 46cm (18in) or desired length.

Work 1 round of St St. Then change to 3.5mm (US 4), 80cm (32in) circular needles and work in rib (k2, P2) for 4cm (1½in).

Cast (bind) off.

CHART

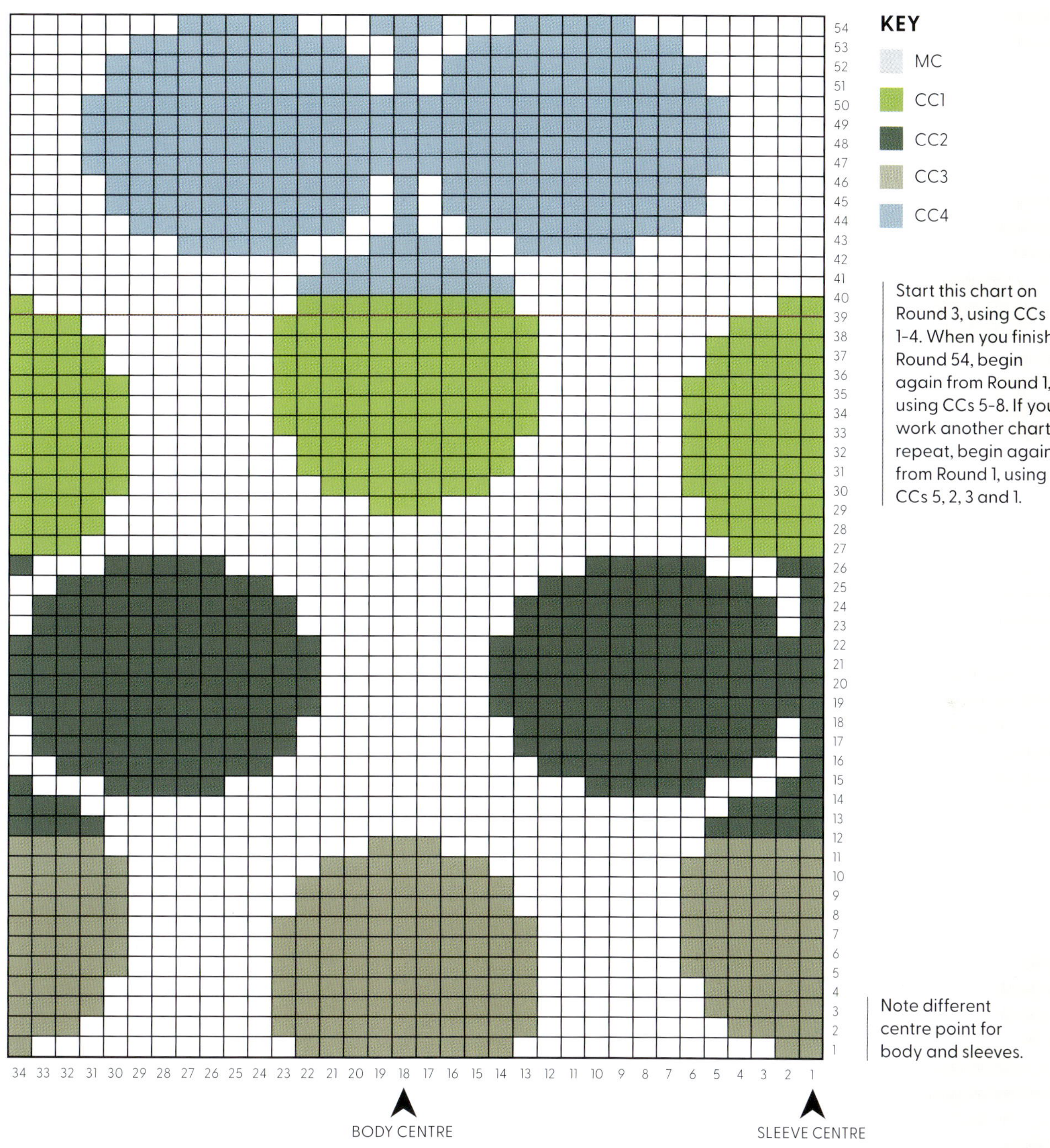

KEY

- MC
- CC1
- CC2
- CC3
- CC4

Start this chart on Round 3, using CCs 1-4. When you finish Round 54, begin again from Round 1, using CCs 5-8. If you work another chart repeat, begin again from Round 1, using CCs 5, 2, 3 and 1.

Note different centre point for body and sleeves.

SLEEVES

Place one set of sleeve sts on 4.5mm (US 7), 40cm (16in) circular needles. Pick up 9 (9) 9 (9) 11 (11) 11 sts from the body sts you cast on for the underarm, and place a marker on each side of the centre underarm st. Work this st in MC on every round.

After 7cm (2¾in), decrease 2 sts every 5 rounds (k2tog before the centre st, ssk after it) until 48 (48) 48 (56) 56 (56) 56 sts remain. Continue without decreasing until the sleeve measures 48cm (19in) or desired length from underarm.

Using MC only, work 1 round of St St, at the same time decreasing to 40 (40) 40 (44) 44 (44) 44 sts, evenly distributing the decreases around.

Change to 3.5mm (US 4) DPNs and work in rib (k2, p2) for 8cm (3¼in), then cast (bind) off. Work the other sleeve in the same way.

FINISHING

Weave in loose ends. Turn the sweater inside out, and fold the neckband in half, with the right side facing you. Use whip stitch to sew the cast-on edge of the neckband loosely to the inside of the neck (see General Techniques: Finishing Techniques for weaving in ends and whip stitch instructions).

To continue the motifs up to the neck on the short row section, embroider the missing sections in duplicate stitch (see General Techniques: Duplicate Stitch) using the chart as a guide.

Place the sweater in a bucket of warm water (no more than 30°C (86°F)) and leave it until fully soaked. Dry flat and stretch into shape. Do not hang the sweater to dry, as this will make it stretch.

Tip

When working very large motifs, it's a good idea to twist the yarns behind the work every four or five stitches. This catches the floating yarn and makes it less likely to catch or pull.

Alternative Colourway

The colours I have used here are:

Main colour (MC)
Rauma Fivel – Yellow 14

Contrast colour (CC)
Rauma Fivel – Natural 01

Suggested other yarns:
Hillesvåg Vidde/Varde/Luna, Novita 7 Brothers/ Hehku, Filcolana Peruvian, or other aran (worsted) weight yarn. Be sure to check the tension (gauge).

MAIKKI
Sweater

I like design and have a penchant for retro; it can be a lamp, an armchair, a dinner set, a piece of clothing ... almost anything. In this pattern, I have tried to capture a feeling of retro in both shape and colour. The name is a tribute to my aunt Maikki, who was very good at needlework, and at choosing a vibrant colour palette.

#maikkisweater

SIZES

1 (2) 3 (4) 5 (6) 7

FINISHED GARMENT MEASUREMENTS

Sleeves:	49cm (19¼in) or desired length
Chest circumference:	85 (89) 97 (106) 115 (124) 133cm 34 (35½) 38½ (42½) 46 (49½) 53in
Body length:	43cm (17in) or desired length from underarm

TENSION (GAUGE)

18 stitches and 24 rows using 4.5mm (US size 7) needles = 10 x 10cm (4 x 4in)

YARN

Aran (worsted) weight yarn

Colours used for this sweater:

Main colour (MC)
Istex Plötulopi – Chocolate 1032

Contrast colour 1 (CC1)
Istex Léttlopi – Apricot 1704

Contrast colour 2 (CC2)
Istex Plötulopi – Sunset Rose 1425

AMOUNT OF YARN

Main colour (MC):	150 (200) 200 (250) 300 (350) 400g 5¼ (7) 7 (8¾) 10½ (12¼) 14oz
Contrast colour 1 (CC1):	200 (250) 250 (300) 350 (400) 450g 7 (8¾) 8¾ (10½) 12¼ (14) 16oz
Contrast colour 2 (CC2):	100 (150) 150 (150) 200 (250) 300g 3½ (5¼) 5¼ (5¼) 7 (8¾) 10½oz

KNITTING NEEDLES

Double pointed needles:	3.5mm (US size 4)
Circular needles:	3.5mm (US size 4) and 4.5mm (US size 7), 40cm (16in)
Circular needles:	4.5mm (US size 7), 60cm (24in)
Circular needles:	3.5mm (US size 4) and 4.5mm (US size 7), 80cm (32in)

YOKE

Using MC and 3.5mm (US 4), 40cm (16in) circular needles, cast on 84 (84) 84 (92) 92 (92) 92 sts. Work in rib (k2, p2) for 4cm (1½in).

Change to 4.5mm (US 7), 60cm, (24in) circular needles and work 1 round of St St, at the same time increasing 8 (8) 8 (16) 16 (16) 16 sts, distributing the increases evenly around.

Place markers according to the table below (see Before You Begin: Construction – Seam Markers). Place a green marker on each side of the first 2 sts (seam 1), and a yellow marker on each side of the 2 sts for seams 2, 3 and 4. Also place a marker on the centre st of each piece to centre the motif (see Before You Begin: Construction – Motif Markers).

Size	Stitches between the markers: (seam 1, back, seam 2, sleeve, seam 3, front, seam 4, sleeve)
1	2, 27, 2, 15, 2, 27, 2, 15 sts
2	2, 27, 2, 15, 2, 27, 2, 15 sts
3	2, 29, 2, 13, 2, 29, 2, 13 sts
4	2, 37, 2, 13, 2, 37, 2, 13 sts
5	2, 37, 2, 13, 2, 37, 2, 13 sts
6	2, 39, 2, 11, 2, 39, 2, 11 sts
3XXL	2, 39, 2, 11, 2, 39, 2, 11 sts

Raglan increase round: *Using MC, k2 seam sts, sm, M1R using correct chart colour for new st, work chart to next marker, M1L using correct chart colour for new st; repeat another 3 times. (8 sts increased around).

Repeat the Raglan increase round every second round until you have 244 (260) 276 (300) 324 (348) 364 sts, ending with an increase round. You will need to change to the 80cm (32in) cable as your stitches increase.

Work 9 more rounds without increases.

You will now divide the piece and work the body and sleeves separately.

Place each set of sleeve sts together with 1 st from the seam on each side onto waste yarn or a stitch holder. Keep the front and back sts and 1 st from the seam on each side on the 4.5mm (US 7), 80cm (32in) circular needle.

BODY (FRONT AND BACK)

Continue working from the chart, casting on 9 (9) 9 (9) 11 (11) 11 sts for each underarm and placing a marker either side of the central underarm st on each side. Work this st in MC on every round.

Continue until the body measures 39cm (15¼in) or desired length from underarm.

Change to 3.5mm (US 4), 80cm (32in) circular needles. Using MC only, work in rib (k2, p2) for 4cm (1½in), then cast (bind) off.

CHART

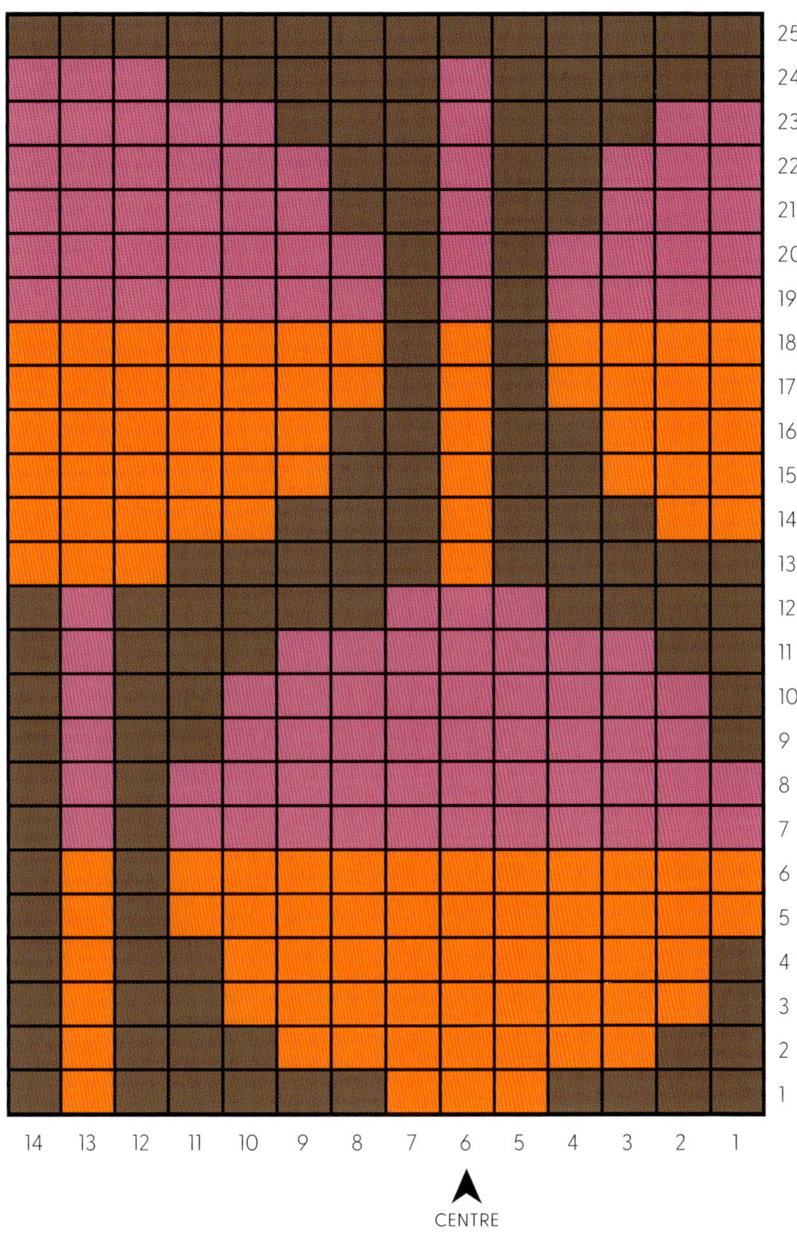

KEY

MC

CC1

CC2

Start this chart on Round 3, using CCs 1-4. When you finish Round 54, begin again from Round 1, using CCs 5-8. If you work another chart repeat, begin again from Round 1, using CCs 5, 2, 3 and 1.

The main pattern has a row of the MC between the lollipop motifs. If you want the motifs to be connected at the top and bottom, as they are in the 3 alternative colourways pictured, only work Rows 1-24 throughout.

The contrast colours used in the Blues/Green Alternative Colourway run in this order:
CC1
CC2
CC3
CC4
CC5
CC6
CC2
CC1
CC4
CC3
CC6
CC5.
Once you have worked them in this order, begin again from CC1, CC2 etc.

SLEEVES

Place one set of sleeve sts on 4.5mm (US 7), 40cm (16in) circular needles. Pick up 9 (9) 9 (9) 11 (11) 11 sts from the body sts you cast on for the underarm, and place a marker on each side of the centre underarm st. Work this st in MC on every round.

Continue working from the chart until sleeve measures 45cm (17¾in) or desired length from underarm.

Using MC only, work 1 round of St St, at the same time decreasing to 40 (40) 40 (44) 44 (44) 44 sts, evenly distributing the decreases around.

Change to 3.5mm (US 4) DPNs. Work in rib (k2, p2) for 4cm (1½in), then cast (bind) off. Work the other sleeve in the same way.

FINISHING

Weave in loose ends (see General Techniques: Finishing Techniques).

Place the sweater in a bucket of warm water (no more than 30°C (86°F)) and leave it until fully soaked. Dry flat and stretch into shape. Do not hang the sweater to dry, as this will make it stretch.

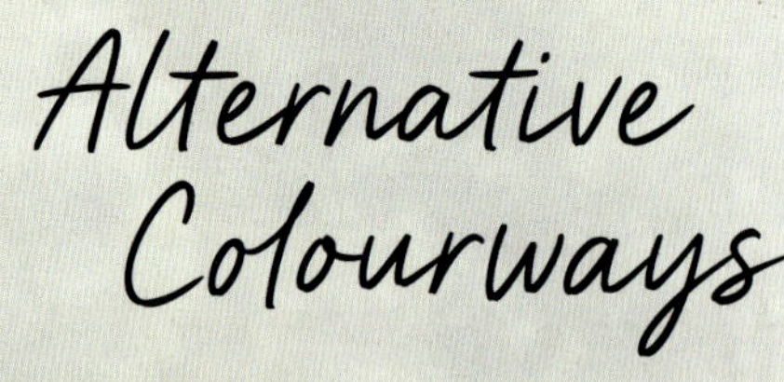

The colours I have used here are:

Blues/Greens

Main colour (MC)
Istex Plötulopi – Blues Blue 2022

Contrast colour 1 (CC1)
Hillesvåg Luna – Mint Green 444

Contrast colour 2 (CC2)
Hillesvåg Vidde – Blue/Gray 324

Contrast colour 3 (CC3)
Hillesvåg Luna – Light Green 446

Contrast colour 4 (CC4)
SKeW Yarns Highland – Alex

Contrast colour 5 (CC5)
Istex Léttlopi – Heaven Blue 1402

Contrast colour 6 (CC6)
Färgkraft Luxus Plus – AquaSoft V

White/Mustard

Main colour (MC)
Järbo Svensk Ull 3-tr – Arctic Fox 59001

Contrast colour (CC)
Järbo Svensk Ull 3-tr – Mustard 59007

White/Burnt orange

Main colour (MC)
Istex Léttlopi – Natural 0051

Contrast colour (CC)
Istex Álafosslopi – Burnt Orange 1236 (split in half)

Suggested other yarns:

Rauma Fivel, Hillesvåg Varde, Novita 7 Brothers, Filcolana Peruvian or other aran (worsted) weight yarn. Be sure to check the tension (gauge).

NORDKAP WINTER *Sweater*

In the summer of 2023 I took an unforgettable trip to the North Cape, the northernmost point of Scandinavia. The weather was completely clear, and the sun shone bright and warm all night. This pattern conveys the extraordinary, magical light of the midnight sun.

#nordkapwintersweater

SIZES

1 (2) 3 (4) 5 (6) 7

FINISHED GARMENT MEASUREMENTS

Sleeves:	48cm (19in) or desired length
Chest circumference:	85 (89) 97 (106) 115 (124) 133cm 34 (35½) 38½ (42½) 46 (49½) 53in
Body length:	46cm (18in) or desired length from underarm

TENSION (GAUGE)

18 stitches and 24 rows using 4.5mm (US size 7) needles = 10 x 10cm (4 x 4in)

YARN

Aran (worsted) weight yarn

Colours used for this sweater:

Main colour (MC)
Istex Plötulopi – Ivory Beige 1038

Contrast colour 1 (CC1)
Istex Plötulopi – Light Beige 0003

Contrast colour 2 (CC2)
Rauma Fivel – Yellow 14

AMOUNT OF YARN

Main colour (MC):	250 (300) 350 (350) 400 (450) 500g 8¾ (10½) 12¼ (12¼) 14 (16) 17¾oz
Contrast colour 1 (CC1):	200 (300) 300 (300) 350 (400) 450g 7 (10½) 10½ (10½) 12¼ (14) 16oz
Contrast colour 2 (CC2):	25g 1oz

KNITTING NEEDLES

Double pointed needles:	3.5mm (US size 4)
Circular needles:	3.5mm (US size 4) and 4.5mm (US size 7), 40cm (16in)
Circular needles:	4.5mm (US size 7), 60cm (24in)
Circular needles:	3.5mm (US size 4) and 4.5mm (US size 7), 80cm (32in)

YOKE

Using MC and 3.5mm (US 4), 40cm (16in) circular needles, cast on 88 (88) 88 (96) 96 (100) 100 sts. Work in rib (k2, p2) for 8cm (3¼in).

Change to 4.5mm (US 7), 60cm (24in) circular needles. Work 1 round of St St, at the same time increasing 4 (4) 4 (12) 12 (8) 8 sts, distributing the increases evenly around. Cut the yarn, ready to work the short-row neck shaping on the back.

Place markers according to the table below (see Before You Begin: Construction – Seam Markers). Place a green marker on each side of the first 2 sts (seam 1), and a yellow marker on each side of the 2 sts for seams 2, 3 and 4.

Size	Stitches between the markers: (seam 1, back, seam 2, sleeve, seam 3, front, seam 4, sleeve)
1	2, 27, 2, 15, 2, 27, 2, 15 sts
2	2, 27, 2, 15, 2, 27, 2, 15 sts
3	2, 29, 2, 13, 2, 29, 2, 13 sts
4	2, 37, 2, 13, 2, 37, 2, 13 sts
5	2, 37, 2, 13, 2, 37, 2, 13 sts
6	2, 39, 2, 11, 2, 39, 2, 11 sts
7	2, 39, 2, 11, 2, 39, 2, 11 sts

NECKLINE WITH SHORT ROWS AT THE NECK

With the right side facing you, rejoin yarn 2 sts before seam 4 and work German Short Rows as follows:

Short row 1: K2, M1R, *sm, k2, sm, M1L, knit to next marker, M1R; repeat from * 2 more times, sm, M1L, k2, turn. You will have worked around to 2 sts after the second seam 3 marker.

Short row 2: DS, purl to second seam 4 marker, sm, p4, turn.

Short row 3: DS, knit to second marker for seam 3, working raglan increases each side of seams as for Short row 1, sm, M1L, k4, turn.

Short row 4: DS, purl to second seam 4 marker, sm, p6. Cut the yarn.

Place a marker on the centre st of each section to centre the motif (see Before You Begin: Construction – Motif Markers).

With the right side facing you, rejoin MC to the first st of seam 1 (between the green markers). Begin working from the chart, making sure it is centred correctly, and working the first Raglan increase round on Round 1 of the chart as follows:

Raglan increase round: *Using MC, k2 seam sts, sm, M1R using correct chart colour for new st, work chart to next marker, M1L using correct chart colour for new st; repeat from * another 3 times. (8 sts increased).

Repeat the Raglan increase round every second round until you have 244 (260) 276 (300) 324 (348) 364 sts, ending with an increase round. You will need to change to the 80cm (32in) cable as your stitches increase.

Continue in pattern for 9 more rounds, working raglan increases only on the sleeves every second round (8 sts increased for each sleeve).

You will now divide the piece and work the body and sleeves separately.

Place each set of sleeve sts together with 1 st from the seam on each side onto waste yarn or a stitch holder. Keep the front and back sts and 1 st from the seam on each side on the 4.5mm (US 7), 80cm (32in) circular needle.

BODY (FRONT AND BACK)

Continue working from the chart, casting on 9 (9) 9 (9) 11 (11) 11 sts for each underarm and placing a marker either side of the central underarm st on each side. Work this st in MC on every round.

Continue until the body measures 42cm (16½in) or desired length from underarm.

Using MC only, work 1 round of St St. If you want a straight rib, like the sweater pictured, increase to 168 (176) 188 (212) 228 (248) 256 sts, distributing the increases evenly around. If you want the rib to tighten a little at the bottom instead, omit these increases.

For both styles, change to 3.5mm (US 4), 80cm (32in) circular needles. Work in rib (K2, P2) for 4cm (1½in), then cast (bind) off.

CHART

KEY

- MC
- CC1
- CC2

When following this chart, work the centre flower sts in MC. The flower centres will be added after the sweater is finished, using CC2 and duplicate stitch.

SLEEVES

Place one set of sleeve sts on 4.5mm (US 7), 40cm (16in) circular needles. Pick up 9 (9) 9 (9) 11 (11) 11 sts from the body sts you cast on for the underarm, and place a marker on each side of the centre underarm st. Work this st in MC on every round.

Continue working from chart until sleeve measures 41cm (16¼in) or desired length from underarm.

Using MC only, work 1 round of St St, at the same time decreasing to 40 (40) 40 (44) 44 (44) 44 sts, evenly distributing the decreases around.

Change to 3.5mm (US 4) DPNs. Work in rib (k2, p2) for 7cm (2¾in), then cast (bind) off. Work the other sleeve in the same way.

FINISHING

Weave in loose ends. Turn the sweater inside out, and fold the neckband in half, with the right side facing you. Use whip stitch to sew the cast-on edge of the neckband loosely to the inside of the neck (see General Techniques: Finishing Techniques for weaving in ends and whip stitch instructions).

To continue the motifs up to the neck on the short row section, embroider the missing sections in duplicate stitch (see General Techniques: Duplicate Stitch) using the chart as a guide.

Place the sweater in a bucket of warm water (no more than 30°C (86°F)) and leave it until fully soaked. Dry flat and stretch into shape. Do not hang the sweater to dry, as this will make it stretch.

Tip

If you wish, you can knit the flower centres using the intarsia technique (not covered in this book), but I recommend adding them with duplicate stitch as it gives the centre of the flower a raised appearance.

Alternative Colourway

The colours I have used here are:

Main colour (MC)
Istex Plötulopi – Sunset Rose 1425

Contrast colour 1 (CC 1)
Istex Plötulopi – Carmine Red 1430

Contrast colour 2 (CC2)
Istex Plötulopi – Wine Red 2027

Suggested other yarns:

Istex Léttlopi, Hillesvåg Vidde/Varde/Luna, Novita 7 Brothers/Icelandic Wool/Hehku, Filcolana Peruvian or other aran (worsted) weight yarn. Be sure to check the tension (gauge).

NORDKAP SUMMER *Sweater*

Like the Nordkap Winter sweater, this pattern represents the amazing light of the midnight sun. It is made using a finer yarn, and its cropped design is a little more feminine than the heavier Nordkap Winter.

#nordkapsummersweater

SIZES

1 (2) 3 (4) 5 (6) 7

FINISHED GARMENT MEASUREMENTS

Sleeves:	39cm (15¼in) or desired length
Chest circumference:	85 (89) 97 (106) 115 (124) 133cm 34 (35½) 38½ (42½) 46 (49½) 53in
Body length:	26cm (10¼in) or desired length from underarm

TENSION (GAUGE)

22 stitches and 30 rows using 3.5mm (US size 4) needles = 10 x 10cm (4 x 4in)

YARN

DK (light worsted) weight yarn

Colours used for this sweater:

Main colour (MC)
Järbo 2-tr Ull – Aqua Ice 74138

Contrast colour 1 (CC1)
Järbo 2-tr Ull – Jade Blue 74141

Contrast colour 2 (CC2)
Järbo 2-tr Ull – Spicy Orange 74119

AMOUNT OF YARN

Main colour (MC):	250 (250) 300 (300) 350 (400) 450g 8¾ (8¾) 10½ (10½) 12¼ (14) 16oz
Contrast colour 1 (CC1):	150 (150) 150 (200) 200 (300) 300g 5¼ (5¼) 5¼ (7) 7 (10½) 10½oz
Contrast colour 2 (CC2):	15 (15) 15 (15) 20 (20) 20g ½ (½) ½ (½) ¾ (¾) ¾oz

KNITTING NEEDLES

Double pointed needles:	3mm (US size 3)
Circular needles:	3mm (US size 3) and 3.5mm (US size 4), 40cm (16in)
Circular needles:	3.5mm (US size 4), 60cm (24in)
Circular needles:	3mm (US size 3) and 3.5mm (US size 4), 80cm (32in)

YOKE

Using MC and 3mm (US 3), 40cm (16in) circular needles, cast on 128 (128) 128 (136) 136 (140) 140 sts. Work in rib (k2, p2) for 4cm (1½in).

Change to 3.5mm (US 4), 60cm (24in) circular needles, and work 1 round of St St. Cut the yarn, ready to work the short-row neck shaping on the back.

Place markers according to the table below (see Before You Begin: Construction – Seam Markers). Place a green marker on each side of the first 2 sts (seam 1), and a yellow marker on each side of the 2 sts for seams 2, 3 and 4.

Size	Stitches between the markers: (seam 1, back, seam 2, sleeve, seam 3, front, seam 4, sleeve)
1	2, 43, 2, 17, 2, 43, 2, 17 sts
2	2, 43, 2, 17, 2, 43, 2, 17 sts
3	2, 43, 2, 17, 2, 43, 2, 17 sts
4	2, 47, 2, 17, 2, 47, 2, 17 sts
5	2, 47, 2, 17, 2, 47, 2, 17 sts
6	2, 49, 2, 17, 2, 49, 2, 17 sts
7	2, 49, 2, 17, 2, 49, 2, 17 sts

NECKLINE WITH SHORT ROWS AT THE NECK

With the right side facing you, rejoin yarn 2 sts before seam 4 and work German Short Rows as follows:

Short row 1: K2, M1R, *sm, k2, sm, M1L, knit to next marker, M1R; repeat from * 2 more times, sm, M1L, k2, turn. You will have worked around to 2 sts after the second seam 3 marker.

Short row 2: DS, purl to second seam 4 marker, sm, p4, turn.

Short row 3: DS, knit to second marker for seam 3, working raglan increases each side of seams as for Short row 1, sm, M1L, k4, turn.

Short row 4: DS, purl to second seam 4 marker, sm, p6. Cut the yarn.

Place a marker on the centre st of each section (see Before You Begin: Construction – Motif Markers).

With the right side facing you, rejoin MC to the first st of seam 1 (between the green markers). Begin working from the chart, making sure it is centred correctly, and working the first Raglan increase round on Round 1 of the chart as follows:

Raglan increase round: *Using MC, k2 seam sts, sm, M1R using correct chart colour for new st, work chart to next marker, M1L using correct chart colour for new st; repeat from * another 3 times. (8 sts increased).

Repeat the Raglan increase round every other round until you have 312 (320) 328 (360) 400 (444) 492 sts, ending with an increase round.

Now continue in pattern without increases until the yoke measures 20 (21) 23 (25) 26 (28) 30cm (7¾ (8¼) 9 (9¾) 10¼ (11) 11¾in) from centre front, including the rib. You will need to change to the 80cm (32in) cable as your sts increase.

You will now divide the piece and work the body and sleeves separately.

Place each set of sleeve sts together with 1 st from the seam on each side onto waste yarn or a stitch holder. Keep the front and back sts and 1 st from the seam on each side on the 3.5mm (US4), 80cm (32in) circular needle.

BODY (FRONT AND BACK)

Continue working from the chart, casting on 7 (7) 7 (9) 9 (9) 9 sts for each underarm and placing a marker either side of the central underarm st on each side. Work this st in MC on every round.

Continue until the body measures 18cm (7in) or desired length from underarm.

Using MC only, work 1 round of St St. If you want a straight rib, like the sweater pictured, increase to 216 (220) 224 (252) 272 (300) 328 sts, distributing the increases evenly around. If you want the rib to tighten a little at the bottom instead, omit these increases.

For both styles, change to 3mm (US 3), 80cm (32in) circular needles. Work in rib (k2, p2) for 8cm (3¼in), then cast (bind) off.

CHART

CENTRE

KEY

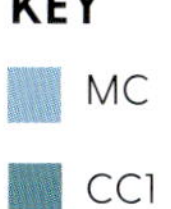

MC

CC1

CC2

When following this chart, work the centre flower sts in MC. The flower centres will be added after the sweater is finished, using CC2 and duplicate stitch.

SLEEVES

Place one set of sleeve sts on 3.5mm (US4), 80cm (32in) circular needles.

Pick up 7 (7) 7 (9) 9 (9) 9 sts from the body sts you cast on for the underarm, and place a marker on each side of the centre underarm st. Work this st in MC on every round.

Continue until sleeve measures 31cm (12¼in) or desired length.

Using MC only, work 1 round of St St.

Change to 3mm (US 3) DPNs. Work in rib (k2, p2) for 8cm (3¼in), then cast (bind) off. Work the other sleeve in the same way.

FINISHING

Weave in loose ends (see General Techniques: Finishing Techniques).

To continue the motifs up to the neck on the short row section, embroider the missing sections in duplicate stitch (see General Techniques: Duplicate Stitch) using the chart as a guide.

Place the sweater in a bucket of warm water (no more than 30°C (86°F)) and leave it until fully soaked. Dry flat and stretch into shape. Do not hang the sweater to dry, as this will make it stretch.

Tip

You can cast on underarm sleeve stitches instead of picking them up from the stitches you cast on for the body. If you do this, you will need to sew up the gap between the body and sleeve after you finish the sweater.

Alternative Colourway

The colours I have used here are:

Main colour (MC)
Rauma Finull – Red Brown 4064

Contrast colour 1 (CC1)
Rauma Finull – Rust Orange 461

Contrast colour 2 (CC2)
Filcolana Saga – Banana 211

Suggested other yarns:

Hillesvåg Tinde/Sol, Novita Nalle or other DK (light worsted) weight yarn. Be sure to check the tension (gauge).

PIRKKO
Sweater

I have loved hearts since I was a little girl; they are symbols of such positivity, and who can say no to love? Hearts make me smile, and smiles are contagious. Imagine what the world could look like if everyone wore sweaters with hearts on them! This sweater is named after another of my wonderful aunts.

#pirkkosweater

SIZES

1 (2) 3 (4) 5 (6) 7

FINISHED GARMENT MEASUREMENTS

Sleeves (short):	18cm (7in) or desired length
Sleeves (long):	48cm (19in) or desired length
Chest circumference:	85 (89) 97 (106) 115 (124) 133cm 34 (35½) 38½ (42½) 46 (49½) 53in
Body length (short):	30cm (11¾in) or desired length from underarm
Body length (long):	43cm (17in) or desired length from underarm

TENSION (GAUGE)

18 stitches and 24 rows using 4.5mm (US size 7) needles = 10 x 10cm (4 x 4in)

YARN

Aran (worsted) weight yarn

Colours used for this sweater:

Main colour (MC) (short-sleeve version)
Istex Plötulopi – Light Beige 0003

Contrast colour (CC) (short-sleeve version)
Istex Plötulopi – White 0001

Main colour (MC) (long-sleeve version)
Hillesvåg Luna – Dark Purple Pink 426

Contrast colour (CC) (long-sleeve version)
Hillesvåg Luna – Coral 427

AMOUNT OF YARN

Main colour (MC) (short version):	100 (100) 150 (200) 300 (300) 300g 3½ (3½) 5¼ (7) 10½ (10½) 10½oz
Contrast colour (CC) (short version):	100 (100) 150 (200) 300 (300) 300g 3½ (3½) 5¼ (7) 10½ (10½) 10½oz
Main colour (MC) (long version):	150 (200) 250 (300) 350 (400) 450g 5¼ (7) 8¾ (10½) 12¼ (14) 16oz
Contrast colour (CC) (long version):	150 (200) 250 (300) 350 (400) 450g 5¼ (7) 8¾ (10½) 12¼ (14) 16oz

KNITTING NEEDLES

Double pointed needles:	3.5mm (US size 4)
Circular needles:	3.5mm (US size 4) and 4.5mm (US size 7), 40cm (16in)
Circular needles:	4.5mm (US size 7), 60cm (24in)
Circular needles:	3.5mm (US size 4) and 4.5mm (US size 7), 80cm (32in)

YOKE

Using MC and 3.5mm (US 4), 40cm (16in) circular needles, cast on 84 (84) 84 (92) 92 (92) 92 sts. Work in rib (k2, p2) for 4cm (1½in).

Change to 4.5mm (US 7), 60cm (24in) circular needles. Work 1 round of St St, at the same time increasing 8 (8) 8 (16) 16 (16) 16 sts, distributing the increases evenly around.

Place markers according to the table below (see Before You Begin: Construction – Seam Markers). Place a green marker on each side of the first 2 sts (seam 1), and a yellow marker on each side of the 2 sts for seams 2, 3 and 4. Also Place a marker on the centre st of each section to centre the motif (see Before You Begin: Construction – Motif Markers).

Size	Stitches between the markers: (seam 1, back, seam 2, sleeve, seam 3, front, seam 4, sleeve)
1	2, 27, 2, 15, 2, 27, 2, 15 sts
2	2, 27, 2, 15, 2, 27, 2, 15 sts
3	2, 29, 2, 13, 2, 29, 2, 13 sts
4	2, 37, 2, 13, 2, 37, 2, 13 sts
5	2, 37, 2, 13, 2, 37, 2, 13 sts
6	2, 39, 2, 11, 2, 39, 2, 11 sts
7	2, 39, 2, 11, 2, 39, 2, 11 sts

Raglan increase round: *Using MC, k2 seam sts, sm, M1R using correct chart colour for new st, work chart to next marker, M1L using correct chart colour for new st; repeat from * another 3 times. (8 sts increased around).

Repeat the Raglan increase round every second round until you have 244 (260) 276 (300) 324 (348) 364 sts, ending with an increase round. You will need to change to the 80cm (32in) cable as your stitches increase.

Work 9 more rounds without increases.

You will now divide the piece and work the body and sleeves separately.

Place each set of sleeve sts together with 1 st from the seam on each side onto waste yarn or a stitch holder. Keep the front and back sts and 1 st from the seam on each side on the 4.5mm (US 7), 80cm (32in) circular needle.

BODY (FRONT AND BACK)

Continue working from the chart, casting on 9 (9) 9 (9) 11 (11) 11 sts for each underarm and placing a marker either side of the central underarm st on each side. Work this st in MC on every round.

Work until the body measures 26cm (10¼in) for the short sweater, or 39cm (15¼in) for the long sweater, or desired length from underarm.

Using MC only, work 1 round of St St.

Change to 3.5mm (US 4), 80cm (32in) circular needles. Work in rib (k2, p2) for 4cm (1½in), then cast (bind) off.

CHARTS

A

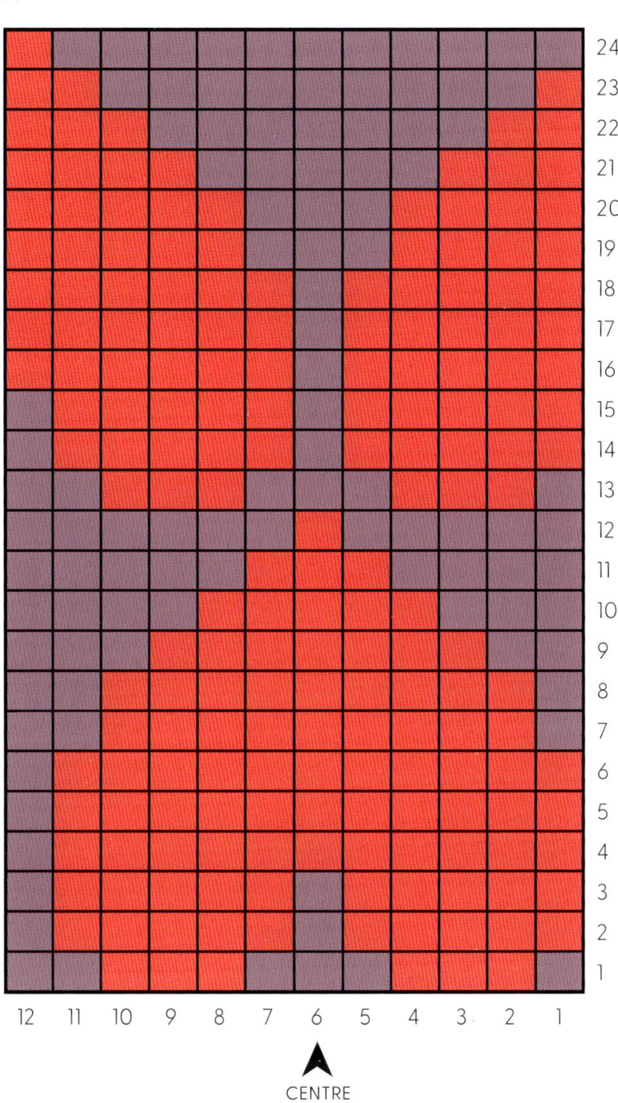

KEY

MC

CC

The contrast colours used in the Alternative Colourway run in this order:
CC1
CC2
CC3

B

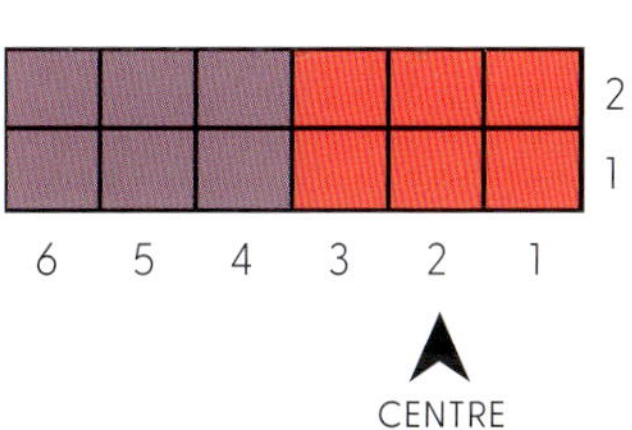

SHORT SLEEVES

Place one set of sleeve sts on 4.5mm (US 7), 40cm (16in) circular needles. Pick up 9 (9) 9 (9) 11 (11) 11 sts from the body sts you cast on for the underarm, and place a marker on each side of the centre underarm st. Work this st in MC on every round.

Continue working from Chart A, or start working Chart B instead, until sleeve measures 13 (13) 14 (14) 14 (15) 15cm (5 (5) 5½ (5½) 5½ (6) 6in) or desired length from underarm.

Using MC only, work 1 round of St St, at the same time decreasing to 52 (52) 56 (56) 56 (60) 60 sts, evenly distributing the decreases around.

Change to 3.5mm (US 4) DPNs. Work in rib (k2, p2) for 4cm (1½in), then cast (bind) off. Work the other sleeve in the same way.

LONG SLEEVES

Place one set of sleeve sts on 4.5mm (US 7), 40cm (16in) circular needles. Pick up 9 (9) 9 (9) 11 (11) 11 sts from the body sts you cast on for the underarm, and place a marker on each side of the centre underarm st. Work this st in MC on every round.

Continue working from Chart A, or start working Chart B instead, until sleeve measures 45cm (17¾in) or desired length.

Change to MC and work 1 round of St St, at the same time decreasing to 40 (40) 40 (44) 44 (44) 48 sts, evenly distributing the decreases around.

Change to 3.5mm (US 4) DPNs. Work in rib (k2, p2) for 4cm (1½in), then cast (bind) off. Work the other sleeve in the same way.

FINISHING

Weave in loose ends (see General Techniques: Finishing Techniques).

Place the sweater in a bucket of warm water (no more than 30°C (86°F)) and leave it until fully soaked. Dry flat and stretch into shape. Do not hang the sweater to dry, as this will make it stretch.

Alternative Colourway

The colours I have used here are:

Main colour (MC)
Hillesvåg Vidde – Natural 300

Contrast colour 1 (CC1)
Hillesvåg Vidde – Light Pink 309

Contrast colour 2 (CC2)
Hillesvåg Vidde – Coral 312

Contrast colour 3 (CC3)
Hillesvåg Vidde – Orange 335

Suggested other yarns:

Istex Léttlopi, Novita 7 Brothers, Hillesvåg Varde, Rauma Fivel or other aran (worsted) weight yarn. Be sure to check the tension (gauge).

SVALBARD *Sweater*

A few years ago, I visited the Svalbard archipelago, which has an Arctic climate that demands warm woollen sweaters. The Svalbard sweater is my interpretation of the island of Spitsbergen, with its green mountainsides lit by the midnight sun in summer, and its peaks capped with snow in winter.

#svalbardsweater

SIZES

1 (2) 3 (4) 5 (6) 7

FINISHED GARMENT MEASUREMENTS

Sleeves:	45cm (17¾in) or desired length
Chest circumference:	85 (89) 97 (106) 115 (124) 133cm 34 (35½) 38½ (42½) 46 (49½) 53in
Body length:	25cm (9¾in) or desired length from underarm

TENSION (GAUGE)

18 stitches and 24 rows using 4.5mm (US size 7) needles = 10 x 10cm (4 x 4in)

YARN

Aran (worsted) weight yarn

Colours used for this sweater:

Main colour (MC)
Istex Léttlopi – White 0051

Contrast colour 1 (CC1)
Filcolana Peruvian – Slightly Purple 369

Contrast colour 2 (CC2)
Filcolana Peruvian – Toxic 269

Contrast colour 3 (CC3)
Rauma Fivel – Yellow 14

AMOUNT OF YARN

Main colour (MC):	300 (300) 350 (375) 400 (425) 475g 10½ (10½) 12¼ (13¼) 14 (15) 16¾oz
Contrast colour 1 (CC1):	150 (150) 175 (200) 225 (250) 275g 5¼ (5¼) 6¼ (7) 8 (8¾) 9¾oz
Contrast colour 2 (CC2):	150 (150) 175 (200) 225 (250) 275g 5¼ (5¼) 6¼ (7) 8 (8¾) 9¾oz
Contrast colour 3 (CC3):	150 (150) 175 (200) 225 (250) 275g 5¼ (5¼) 6¼ (7) 8 (8¾) 9¾oz

KNITTING NEEDLES

Circular needles:	3.5mm (US size 4) and 4.5mm (US size 7), 40cm (16in)
Circular needles:	4.5mm (US size 7), 60cm (24in)
Circular needles:	3.5mm (US size 4) and 4.5mm (US size 7), 80cm (32in)

YOKE

Using MC and 3.5mm (US 4), 40cm (16in) circular needles, cast on 88 (88) 88 (96) 96 (100) 100 sts. Work in rib (k2, p2) for 8cm (3¼in).

Change to 4.5mm (US 7), 60cm (24in) circular needles and work 1 round of St St, at the same time increasing 4 (4) 4 (12) 12 (8) 8 sts distributing the increases evenly around. Cut the yarn, ready to work the short-row neck shaping on the back.

Place markers according to the table below (see Before You Begin: Construction – Seam Markers). Place a green marker on each side of the first 2 sts (seam 1), and a yellow marker on each side of the 2 sts for seams 2, 3 and 4.

Size	Stitches between the markers: (seam 1, back, seam 2, sleeve, seam 3, front, seam 4, sleeve)
1	2, 27, 2, 15, 2, 27, 2, 15 sts
2	2, 27, 2, 15, 2, 27, 2, 15 sts
3	2, 29, 2, 13, 2, 29, 2, 13 sts
4	2, 37, 2, 13, 2, 37, 2, 13 sts
5	2, 37, 2, 13, 2, 37, 2, 13 sts
6	2, 39, 2, 11, 2, 39, 2, 11 sts
7	2, 39, 2, 11, 2, 39, 2, 11 sts

NECKLINE WITH SHORT ROWS AT THE NECK

With the right side facing you, rejoin yarn 2 sts before seam 4 and work German Short Rows as follows:

Short row 1: K2, M1R, *sm, k2, sm, M1L, knit to next marker, M1R; repeat from * 2 more times, sm, M1L, k2, turn. You will have worked around to 2 sts after the second seam 3 marker.

Short row 2: DS, purl to second seam 4 marker, sm, p4, turn.

Short row 3: DS, knit to second marker for seam 3, working raglan increases each side of seams as for Short row 1, sm, M1L, k4, turn.

Short row 4: DS, purl to second seam 4 marker, sm, p6. Cut the yarn.

Place a marker on the centre st of each section to centre the motif (see Before You Begin: Construction – Motif Markers).

With the right side facing you, rejoin MC to the first st of seam 1 (between the green markers). Begin working from the chart, making sure it is centred correctly, and working the first Raglan increase round on Round 1 of the chart as follows:

Raglan increase round: *Using MC, k2 seam sts, sm, M1R using correct chart colour for new st, work chart to next marker, M1L using correct chart colour for new st; repeat from * another 3 times. (8 sts increased).

Repeat the Raglan increase round every second round until you have 244 (260) 276 (300) 324 (348) 364 sts, ending with an increase round. You will need to change to the 80cm (32in) cable as your stitches increase.

Continue in pattern for 9 more rounds, working raglan increases only on the sleeves every second round (8 sts increased for each sleeve).

You will now divide the piece and work the body and sleeves separately.

Place each set of sleeve sts together with 1 st from the seam on each side onto waste yarn or a stitch holder. Keep the front and back sts and 1 st from the seam on each side on the 4.5mm (US 7), 80cm (32in) circular needle.

BODY (FRONT AND BACK)

Continue working from the chart, casting on 9 (9) 9 (9) 11 (11) 11 sts for each underarm and placing a marker either side of the central underarm st on each side. Work this st in MC on every round.

Continue until the body measures 20cm (7¾in) or desired length from underarm.

Using MC only, work 1 round of St St. If you want a straight rib, as on the sweater pictured, increase to 168 (176) 188 (212) 228 (248) 256 sts, distributing the increases evenly around. If you want the rib to tighten a little at the bottom instead, omit these increases.

For both styles, change to 3.5mm (US 4), 80cm (32in) circular needles.

Change to CC2 and work in rib (k2, p2) for 5cm (2in), then cast (bind) off.

CHART

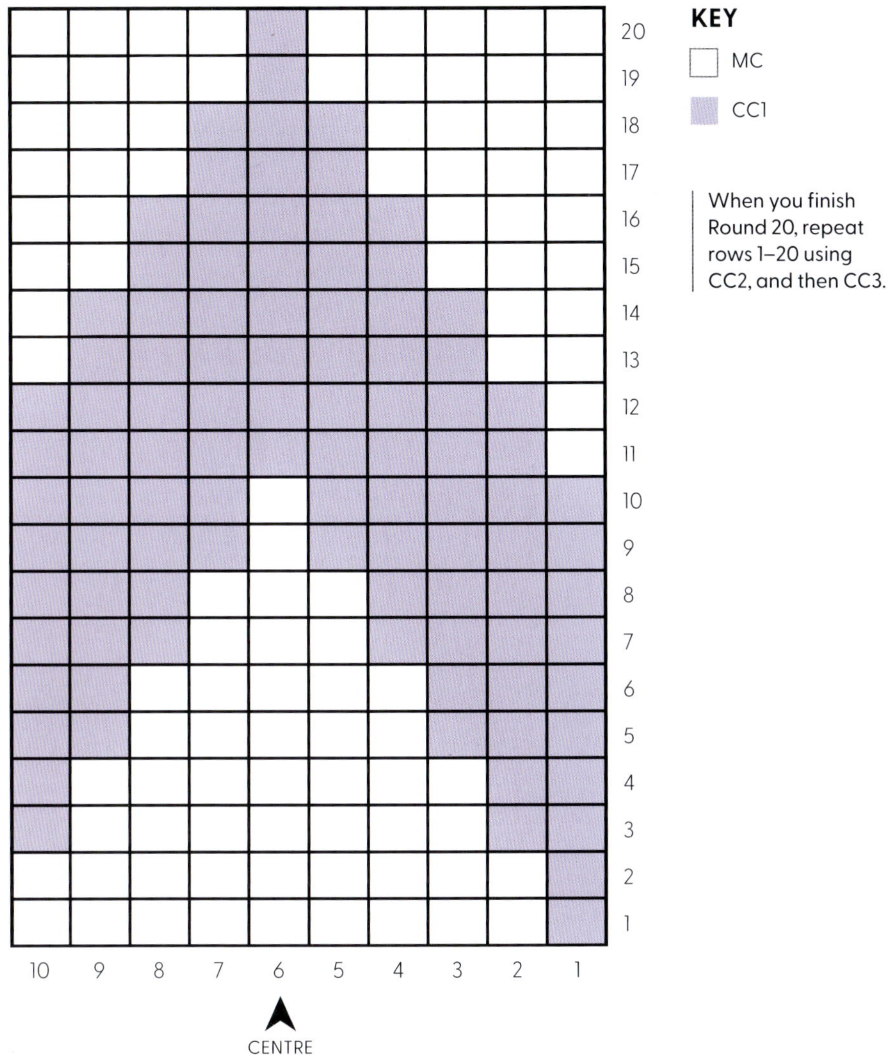

KEY

MC

CC1

When you finish Round 20, repeat rows 1–20 using CC2, and then CC3.

SLEEVES

Place one set of sleeve sts on 4.5mm (US 7), 40cm (16in) circular needles. Pick up 9 (9) 9 (9) 11 (11) 11 sts from the body sts you cast on for the underarm, and place a marker on each side of the centre underarm st. Work this st in MC on every round.

Continue until sleeve measures 38cm (15in) or desired length from underarm.

Using MC only, work 1 round of St St, at the same time increasing to 80 (84) 88 (88) 96 (100) 104 sts, evenly distributing the increases around.

Change to CC1 and 3.5mm (US 4), 40cm (16in) circular needles. Work in rib (k2, p2) for 7cm (2¾in), then cast (bind) off. Work the other sleeve in the same way.

FINISHING

Weave in loose ends. Turn the sweater inside out, and fold the neckband in half, with the right side facing you. Use whip stitch to sew the cast-on edge of the neckband loosely to the inside of the neck (see General Techniques: Finishing Techniques for weaving in ends and whip stitch instructions).

To continue the motifs up to the neck on the short row section, embroider the missing sections in duplicate stitch (see General Techniques: Duplicate Stitch) using the chart as a guide.

Place the sweater in a bucket of warm water (no more than 30°C (86°F)) and leave it until fully soaked. Dry flat and stretch into shape. Do not hang the sweater to dry, as this will make it stretch.

Tip

When you remove the finished sweater from its soaking water, gently squeeze out the water by rolling it in a dry towel before you lay it out.

Alternative Colourway

The colours I have used here are:

Main colour (MC)
Filcolana Peruvian – Ballerina 318

Contrast colour (CC)
Filcolana Peruvian – Carrot 215

Suggested other yarns:

Istex Plötulopi, Hillesvåg Vidde/Varde/Luna, Novita Icelandic Wool/7 Brothers or other aran (worsted) weight yarn. Be sure to check the tension (gauge).

TOINI WINTER *Sweater*

When I was around five I learned to crochet, which first opened the door to my creativity. My aunt Toini was one of the people who taught me. I have filled this pattern with flowers to remind me of a Scandinavian wildflower meadow, scattered with colour as far as the eye can see.

#toiniwintersweater

SIZES

1 (2) 3 (4) 5 (6) 7

FINISHED GARMENT MEASUREMENTS

Sleeves:	49cm (19¼in) or desired length
Chest circumference:	85 (89) 97 (106) 115 (124) 133cm 34 (35½) 38½ (42½) 46 (49½) 53in
Body length:	43cm (17in) or desired length from underarm

TENSION (GAUGE)

18 stitches and 24 rows using 4.5mm (US size 7) needles = 10 x 10cm (4 x 4in)

YARN

Aran (worsted) weight yarn

Colours used for this sweater:

Main colour (MC)
Istex Plötulopi – Golden Blush 2028

Contrast colour (CC)
Istex Plötulopi – Sunset Rose 1425

AMOUNT OF YARN

Main colour (MC):	150 (200) 200 (250) 250 (300) 350 5¼ (7) 7 (8¾) 8¾ (10½) 12¼oz
Contrast colour (CC):	150 (200) 200 (250) 250 (300) 350 5¼ (7) 7 (8¾) 8¾ (10½) 12¼oz

KNITTING NEEDLES

Double pointed needles:	3.5mm (US size 4)
Circular needles:	3.5mm (US size 4) and 4.5mm (US size 7), 40cm (16in)
Circular needles:	4.5mm (US size 7), 60cm (24in)
Circular needles:	3.5mm (US size 4) and 4.5mm (US size 7), 80cm (32in)

YOKE

Using MC and 3.5mm (US 4), 40cm (16in) circular needles, cast on 84 (84) 84 (92) 92 (92) 92 sts. Work in rib (k2, p2) for 4cm (1½in).

Change to 4.5mm (US 7), 60cm, (24in) circular needles, and work 1 round of St St, at the same time increasing 8 (8) 8 (16) 16 (16) 16 sts, distributing the increases evenly around.

Place markers according to the table below (see Before You Begin: Construction – Seam Markers). Place a green marker on each side of the first 2 sts (seam 1), and a yellow marker on each side of the 2 sts for seams 2, 3 and 4. Also Place a marker on the centre st of each section to centre the motif (see Before You Begin: Construction – Motif Markers).

Size	Stitches between the markers: (seam 1, back, seam 2, sleeve, seam 3, front, seam 4, sleeve)
1	2, 27, 2, 15, 2, 27, 2, 15 sts
2	2, 27, 2, 15, 2, 27, 2, 15 sts
3	2, 29, 2, 13, 2, 29, 2, 13 sts
4	2, 37, 2, 13, 2, 37, 2, 13 sts
5	2, 37, 2, 13, 2, 37, 2, 13 sts
6	2, 39, 2, 11, 2, 39, 2, 11 sts
7	2, 39, 2, 11, 2, 39, 2, 11 sts

Begin working from either chart A or chart B, making sure it is centred correctly, and working the first Raglan increase round on Round 1 of the chart as follows:

Raglan increase round: *Using MC, k2 seam sts, sm, M1R using correct chart colour for new st, work chart to next marker, M1L using correct chart colour for new st; repeat from * another 3 times. (8 sts increased).

Repeat the Raglan increase round every second round until you have 244 (260) 276 (300) 324 (348) 364 sts, ending with an increase round.

Work 9 more rounds without increases.

You will now divide the piece and work the body and sleeves separately.

Place each set of sleeve sts together with 1 st from the seam on each side onto waste yarn or a stitch holder. Keep the front and back sts and 1 st from the seam on each side on the 4.5mm (US 7), 80cm (32in) circular needle.

BODY (FRONT AND BACK)

Continue working from the chart, casting on 9 (9) 9 (9) 11 (11) 11 sts for each underarm and placing a marker either side of the central underarm st on each side. Work this st in MC on every round.

Continue until the body measures 39cm (15¼in) or desired length from underarm.

Change to 3.5mm (US 4), 80cm (32in) circular needles. Using MC only, work 1 round of St St.

Work in rib (k2, p2) for 4cm (1½in), then cast (bind) off.

CHARTS

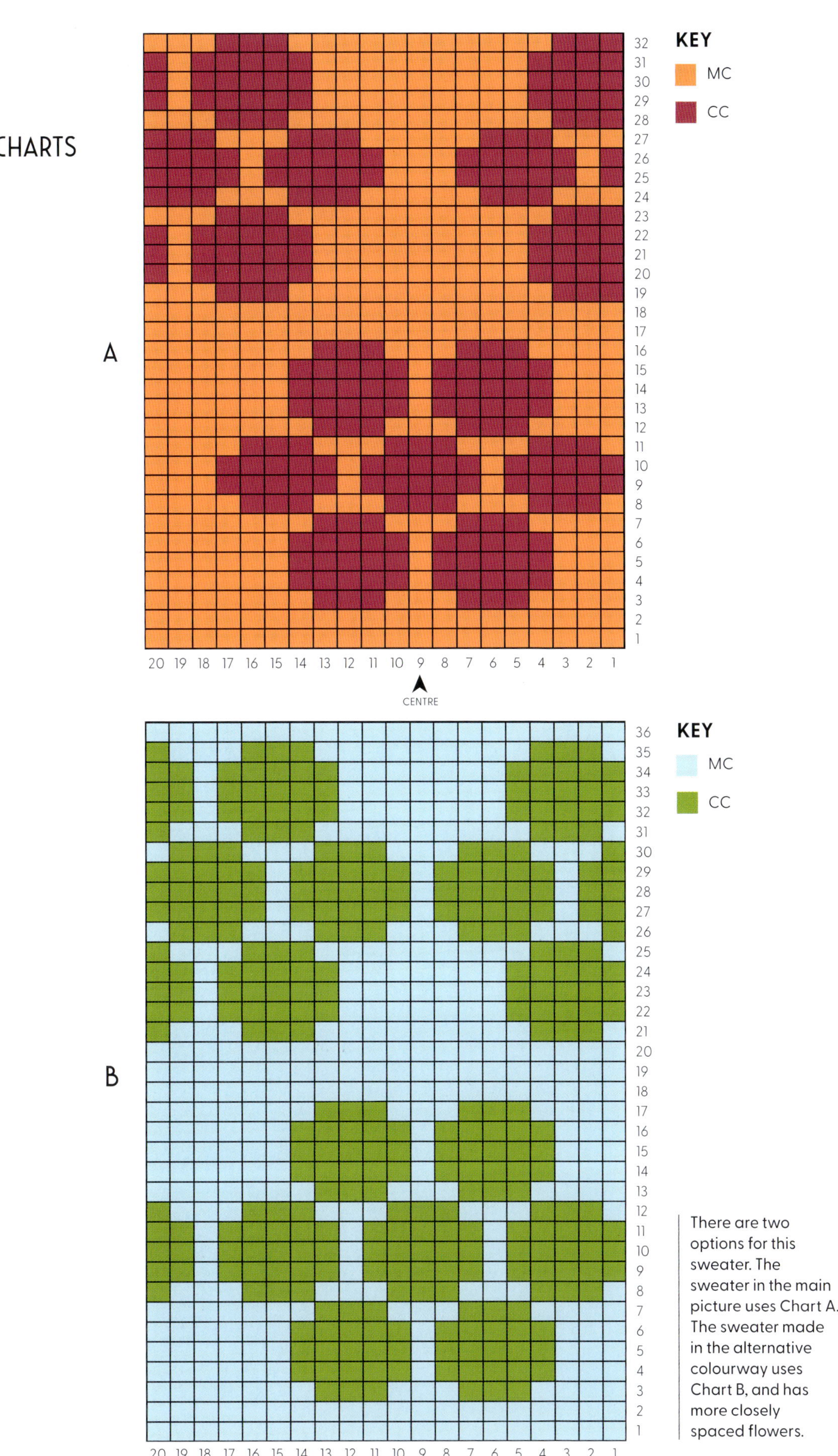

There are two options for this sweater. The sweater in the main picture uses Chart A. The sweater made in the alternative colourway uses Chart B, and has more closely spaced flowers.

SLEEVES

Place one set of sleeve sts on 4.5mm (US 7), 40cm (16in) circular needles. Pick up 9 (9) 9 (9) 11 (11) 11 sts from the body sts you cast on for the underarm, and place a marker on each side of the centre underarm st. Work this st in MC on every round.

Continue working from chart until sleeve measures 45cm (17¾in) or desired length.

Using MC only, work 1 round of St St, at the same time decreasing to 40 (40) 40 (44) 44 (44) 44 sts, evenly distributing the decreases around.

Change to 3.5mm (US 4) DPNs. Work in rib (k2, p2) for 4cm (1½in), then cast (bind) off. Work the other sleeve in the same way.

FINISHING

Weave in loose ends (see General Techniques: Finishing Techniques).

Place the sweater in a bucket of warm water (no more than 30°C (86°F)) and leave it until fully soaked. Dry flat and stretch into shape. Do not hang the sweater to dry, as this will make it stretch.

Alternative Colourway

The colours I have used here are:

Main colour (MC)
Filcolana Peruvian – Sea Foam 333

Contrast colour (CC)
Filcolana Peruvian – Sprout 379

Suggested other yarns:

Rauma Finull, Hillesvåg Tinde/Sol, Novita Nalle or other aran (worsted) weight yarn. Be sure to check the tension (gauge).

This version was knitted using chart B.

TOINI SUMMER *Sweater*

Just like the Toini Winter sweater, this design was inspired by flower-filled Scandinavian meadows. This version is more suitable for warmer weather. It is waist length with short sleeves, and is made with a finer, more lightweight yarn.

#toinisummersweater

SIZES

1 (2) 3 (4) 5 (6) 7

FINISHED GARMENT MEASUREMENTS

Sleeves:	13cm (5in) or desired length
Chest circumference:	85 (89) 97 (106) 115 (124) 133cm 34 (35½) 38½ (42½) 46 (49½) 53in
Body length:	29cm (11½in) or desired length from underarm

TENSION (GAUGE)

22 stitches and 30 rows using 3.5mm (US size 4) needles = 10 x 10cm (4 x 4in)

YARN

DK (light worsted) weight yarn

Colours used for this sweater:

Main colour (MC)
Järbo 2-tr Ull – Young Leaves 74146

Contrast colour (CC)
Järbo 2-tr Ull – Apple Blossom 74125

AMOUNT OF YARN

Main colour (MC):	200 (200) 250 (250) 300 (300) 350g 7 (7) 8¾ (8¾) 10½ (10½) 12¼oz
Contrast colour (CC):	150 (150) 200 (200) 200 (300) 300g 5¼ (5¼) 7 (7) 7 (10½) 10½oz

KNITTING NEEDLES

Double pointed needles:	3mm (US size 3)
Circular needles:	3mm (US size 3) and 3.5mm (US size 4), 40cm (16in)
Circular needles:	3.5mm (US size 4), 60cm (24in)
Circular needles:	3mm (US size 3) and 3.5mm (US size 4), 80cm (32in)

YOKE

Using CC and 3mm (US 3), 40cm (16in) circular needles, cast on 128 (128) 128 (136) 136 (140) 140 sts. Work 5 rounds of St St.

Change to MC and work 1 round of St St, then work in rib (k2, p2) for 5cm (2in).

Change to 3.5mm (US 4), 60cm (24in) circular needles and work 1 round of St St. Cut the yarn, ready to work the short-row neck shaping on the back.

Place markers according to the table below (see Before You Begin: Construction – Seam Markers). Place a green marker on each side of the first 2 sts (seam 1), and a yellow marker on each side of the 2 sts for seams 2, 3 and 4.

Size	Stitches between the markers: (seam 1, back, seam 2, sleeve, seam 3, front, seam 4, sleeve)
1	2, 43, 2, 17, 2, 43, 2, 17 sts
2	2, 43, 2, 17, 2, 43, 2, 17 sts
3	2, 43, 2, 17, 2, 43, 2, 17 sts
4	2, 47, 2, 17, 2, 47, 2, 17 sts
5	2, 47, 2, 17, 2, 47, 2, 17 sts
6	2, 49, 2, 17, 2, 49, 2, 17 sts
7	2, 49, 2, 17, 2, 49, 2, 17 sts

NECKLINE WITH SHORT ROWS AT THE NECK

With the right side facing you, rejoin yarn 2 sts before seam 4 and work German Short Rows as follows:

Short row 1: K2, M1R, *sm, k2, sm, M1L, knit to next marker, M1R; repeat from * 2 more times, sm, M1L, k2, turn. You will have worked around to 2 sts after the second seam 3 marker.

Short row 2: DS, purl to second seam 4 marker, sm, p4, turn.

Short row 3: DS, knit to second marker for seam 3, working raglan increases each side of seams as for Short row 1, sm, M1L, k4, turn.

Short row 4: DS, purl to second seam 4 marker, sm, p6. Cut the yarn.

Place a marker on the centre st of each section (see Before You Begin: Construction – Motif Markers).

With the right side facing you, rejoin MC to the first st of seam 1 (between the green markers). Begin working from the chart, making sure it is centred correctly, and working the first Raglan increase round on Round 1 of the chart as follows:

Raglan increase round: *Using MC, k2 seam sts, sm, M1R using correct chart colour for new st, work chart to next marker, M1L using correct chart colour for new st; repeat from * another 3 times. (8 sts increased).

Repeat the Raglan increase round every second round until you have 312 (320) 328 (360) 400 (444) 492 sts. You will need to change to the 80cm (32in) cable as your stitches increase.

Now work additional rounds without increases until the yoke measures 20 (21) 23 (25) 26 (28) 30cm (7¾ (8¼) 9 (9¾) 10¼ (11) 11¾in) from centre front, including the rib.

You will now divide the piece and work the body and sleeves separately.

Place each set of sleeve sts together with 1 st from the seam on each side onto waste yarn or a stitch holder Keep the front and back sts and 1 st from the seam on each side on the 4.5mm (US 7), 80cm (32in) circular needle.

BODY (FRONT AND BACK)

Continue working from the chart, casting on 7 (7) 7 (9) 9 (9) 9 sts for each underarm and placing a marker either side of the central underarm st on each side. Work this st in MC on every round.

Continue until the body measures 23cm (9in) or desired length from underarm.

Change to 3mm (US 3), 80cm (32in) circular needles. Using MC only, work in rib (k2, p2) for 5cm (2in), then work 1 round of St St.

Change to CC and work 5 rounds of St St, then cast (bind) off.

CHART

36
35
34
33
32
31
30
29
28
27
26
25
24
23
22
21
20
19
18
17
16
15
14
13
12
11
10
9
8
7
6
5
4
3
2
1
20 19 18 17 16 15 14 13 12 11 10 9 8 7 6 5 4 3 2 1
CENTRE
KEY
MC
CC1

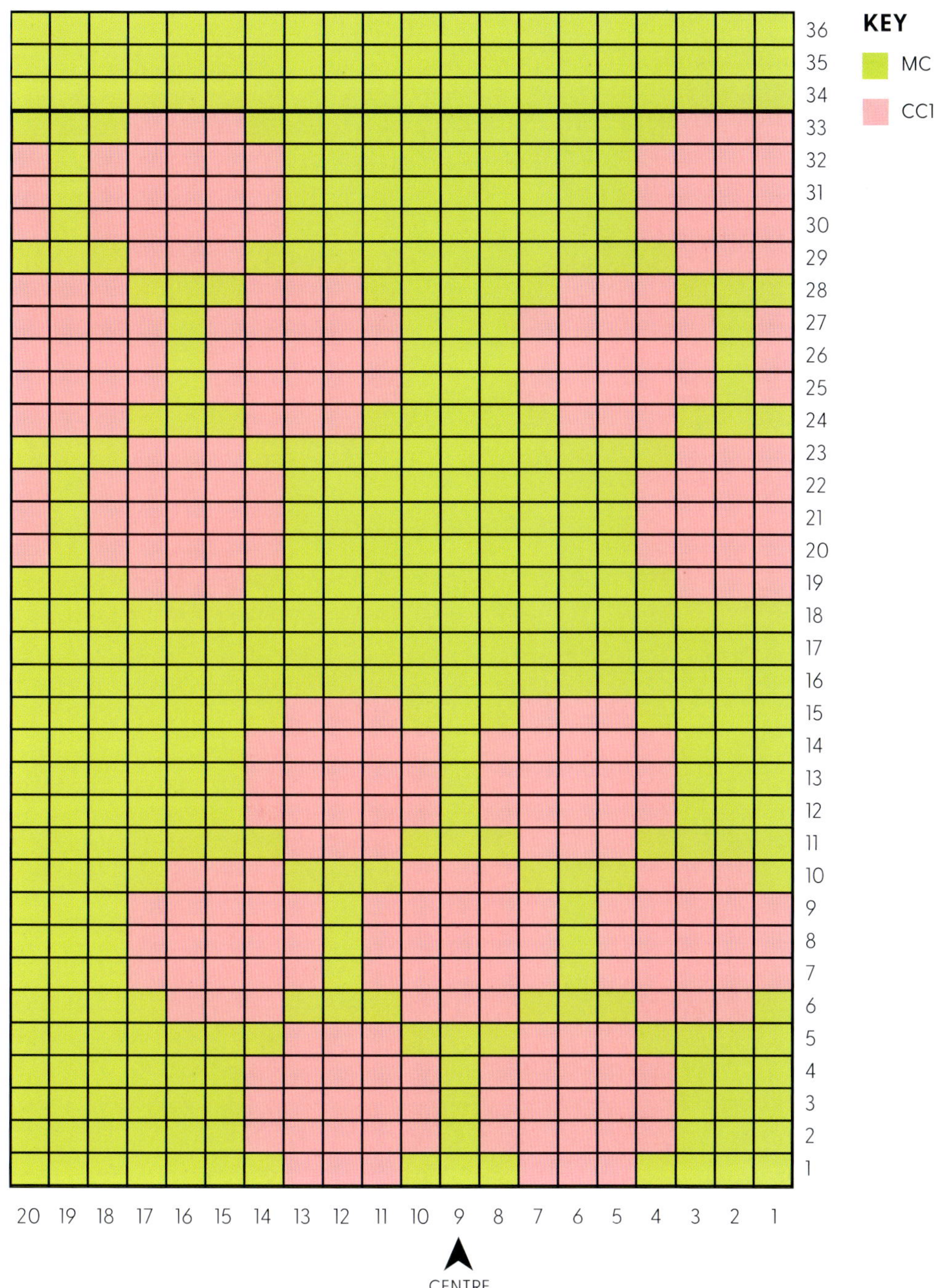

SLEEVES

Place one set of sleeve sts on 3.5mm (US 4), 40cm (16in) circular needles. Pick up 7 (7) 7 (9) 9 (9) 9 sts from the body sts you cast on for the underarm, and place a marker on each side of the centre underarm st. Work this st in MC on every round.

Continue working from chart until sleeve measures 9cm (3½in) or desired length from underarm.

Using MC only, work 1 round of St St, at the same time decreasing to 60 (64) 64 (68) 68 (72) 72 sts, evenly distributing the decreases around.

Change to 3mm (US 3) DPNs. Work in rib (k2, p2) for 3cm (1¼in), then work 1 round of St St.

Change to CC. Work 5 rounds of St St, then cast (bind) off. Work the other sleeve in the same way.

FINISHING

Weave in loose ends (see General Techniques: Finishing Techniques).

To continue the motifs up to the neck on the short row section, embroider the missing sections in duplicate stitch (see General Techniques: Duplicate Stitch) using the chart as a guide.

Place the sweater in a bucket of warm water (no more than 30°C (86°F)) and leave it until fully soaked. Dry flat and stretch into shape. Do not hang the sweater to dry, as this will make it stretch.

Tip

If you wish, you can add shaping to the body by decreasing 1 stitch on each side of the side seams every few rows until the body is the size you want. Keep trying the sweater on as you go to make sure the fit is right.

Alternative Colourway

The colours I have used here are:

Main colour (MC)
Filcolana Saga – Coral 254

Contrast colour (CC)
Filcolana Saga – Fandango 118

Suggested other yarns:

Rauma Finull, Hillesvåg Tinde/Sol, Novita Nalle or other DK (light worsted) weight yarn. Be sure to check the tension (gauge).

GENERAL TECHNIQUES

BASIC STITCHES

SLIP KNOT

This knot attaches the yarn to the needle.

1. Make a loop in the yarn near the end (A).
2. Bring the ball end of the yarn under the loop and use the tip of the needle to pull it to the front (B).
3. Pull both ends of the yarn to secure the knot around the needle. Do not pull too tightly. Leave the slip knot slightly loose (C).

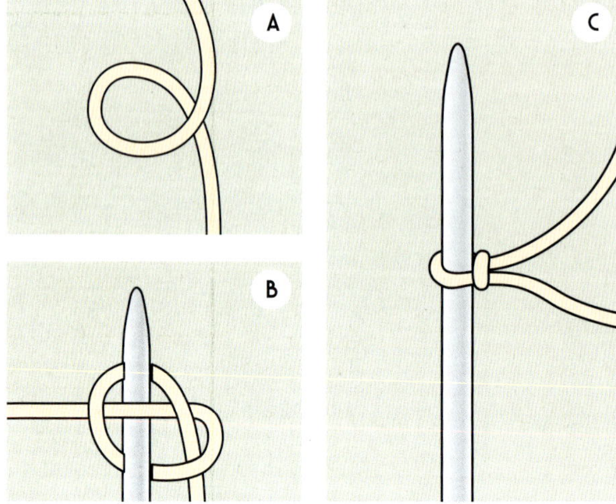

LONG-TAIL CAST ON

This method creates an elastic edge suitable for stitches or yarns without much stretch.

1. Measure out about 2.5cm (1in) of yarn for each stitch to be made. Make a slip knot on the left-hand needle at the end of the measured yarn. Wrap the ball end of the yarn around the index finger and the tail end around the thumb (D).
2. Insert the tip of the right-hand needle up through the loop on the thumb (E).
3. Catch the loop of yarn on the index finger and pull through the loop on the thumb (F).
4. Drop the loop from the thumb and pull tight to form a stitch on the needle (G).

Repeat these steps until you have the required number of stitches.

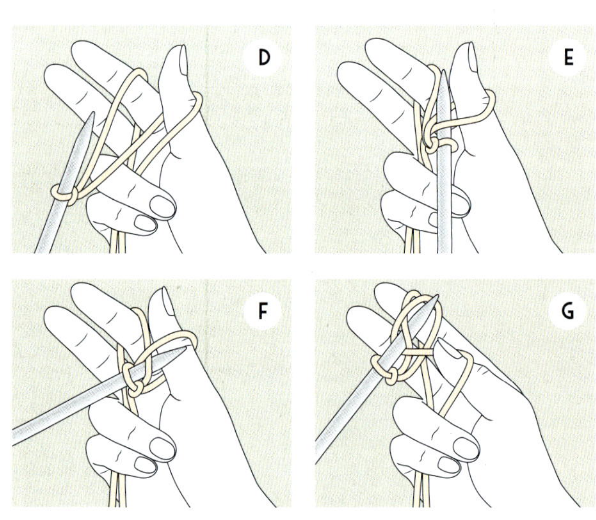

KNIT STITCH ENGLISH (K)

With the English method the yarn is held in the right hand, at the back of the work for the knit stitch.

1. Hold the needle with the stitches to be worked in your left hand, with the working yarn at the back. Insert the tip of the right-hand needle into the first stitch from front to back and left to right (A).
2. Take the yarn behind and around the right-hand needle from left to right (B).
3. Use the tip of the right-hand needle to pull the loop through the stitch on the left-hand needle to form a new stitch on the right-hand needle (C).
4. Slide stitch off the left-hand needle (D).

Repeat these steps for every knit stitch.

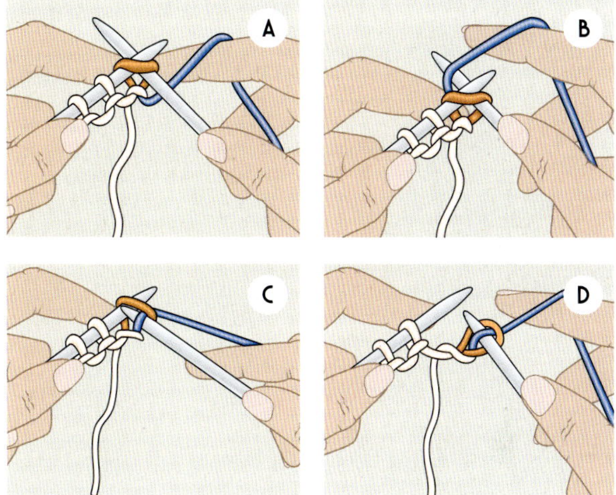

KNIT STITCH CONTINENTAL (K)

With the Continental method the yarn is wrapped around the index finger of the left hand, at the back of the work for the knit stitch.

1. Insert the tip of the right-hand needle into the first stitch from front to back and left to right (E).
2. Take the yarn in front of and around the right-hand needle from left to right (F).
3. Use the tip of the right-hand needle to pull the loop through the stitch on the left-hand needle to form a new stitch on the right-hand needle (G).
4. Slide the stitch off the left-hand needle (H).

Repeat these steps for every knit stitch.

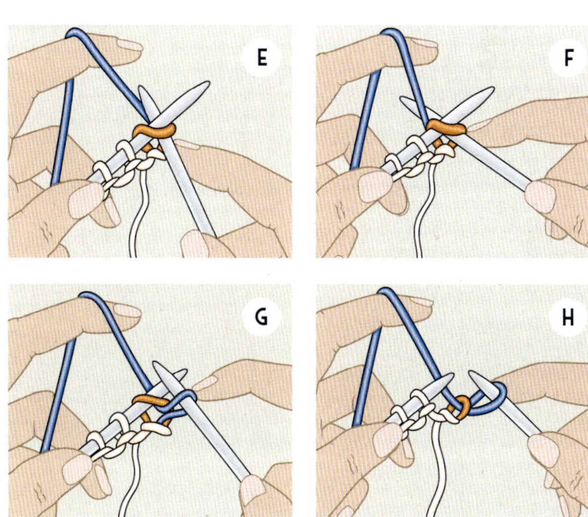

PURL STITCH ENGLISH (P)

With the English method the yarn is held in the right hand, at the front of the work for the purl stitch.

1. Hold the needle with the stitches to be worked in your left hand, with the yarn at the front. Insert the tip of the right-hand needle into the front of the first stitch from right to left (A).
2. Take the yarn in front of and around the right-hand needle to form the next stitch (B).
3. Use the tip of the right-hand needle to pull the loop through the stitch on the left-hand needle to form a new stitch on the right-hand needle (C).
4. Slide the stitch off the left-hand needle (D).

Repeat these steps for every purl stitch.

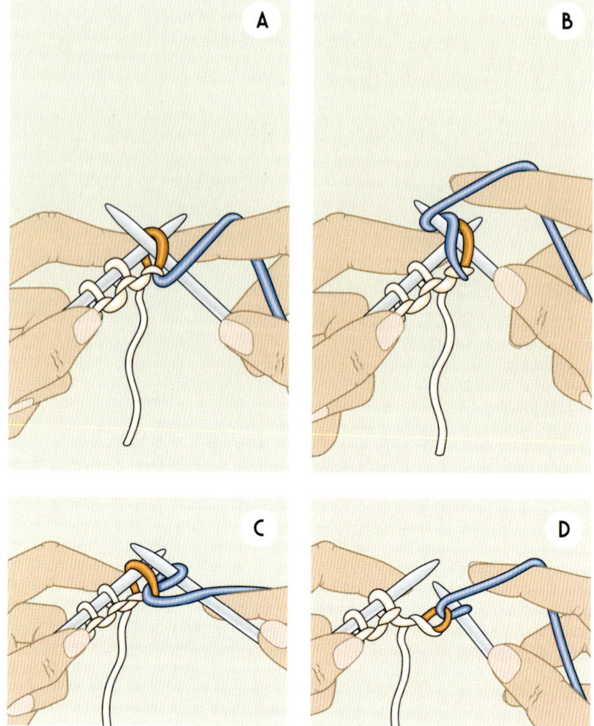

PURL STITCH CONTINENTAL (P)

With the Continental method the yarn is wrapped around the index finger of the left hand, at the front of the work for the purl stitch.

1. Hold the needle with the stitches in your left hand, with the yarn at the front. Insert the tip of the right-hand needle into the front of the first stitch from right to left (E).
2. Take the yarn over and behind the right-hand needle to form the next stitch (F).
3. Use the tip of the right-hand needle to pull the loop through the stitch on the left-hand needle to form a new stitch on the right-hand needle (G).
4. Slide the stitch off the left-hand needle (H).

Repeat these steps for every purl stitch.

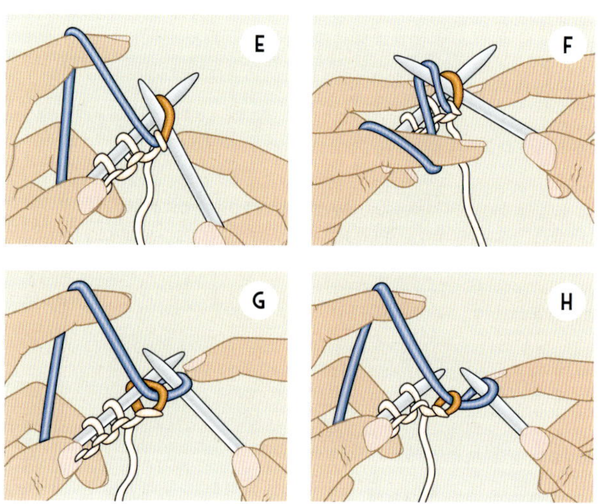

WORKING IN THE ROUND

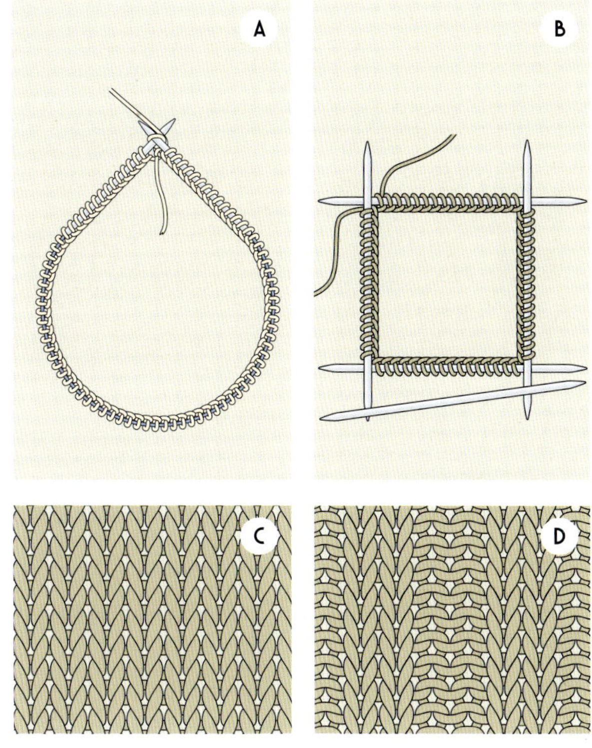

1. When working with a large number of stitches, work in the round on circular needles. Use a longer cord the more stitches you have so as not to stretch the work (A).
2. When working with small circumferences, like sleeves, it's better to use a set of double-pointed needles (B).
3. To work St St in the round, every round will be knitted (C).
4. To work k2, p2 rib in the round, you need an even number of stitches, divisible by 4. You will always knit the k stitches and purl the p stitches (D).

GERMAN SHORT ROWS

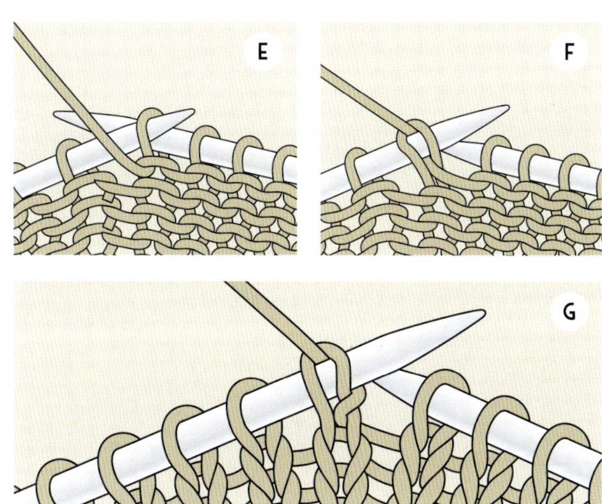

With this technique you work in rows over only part of the round to create extra fabric in just one area.

1. When working a short row on the right side (wrong side), knit (purl) to the stitch specified in the pattern. Turn the work, make sure the yarn is at the front of the work and slip the next stitch from the left-hand needle to the right-hand needle (E).
2. Pull the yarn to the back over the top of the needle – this will make the stitch look like 2 stitches – a 'double stitch', or DS. (F shows a DS on the wrong side of the work, and G shows a DS on the right side.) Bring the yarn to the front between the needles to start purling (knitting) as normal on the next row.
3. When you return to knitting in the round, every time you reach a DS, knit the two legs of the stitch together as one stitch. This closes up the gap made by turning in the middle of the row.

INCREASE AND DECREASE

MAKE ONE LEFT (M1L)

This technique creates a left-leaning 1-stitch knit increase.

1. Insert the left-hand needle from front to back into the bar between the stitches on each needle, and slip it onto the needle (A).

2. Knit into the back of the loop, creating an extra stitch (B).

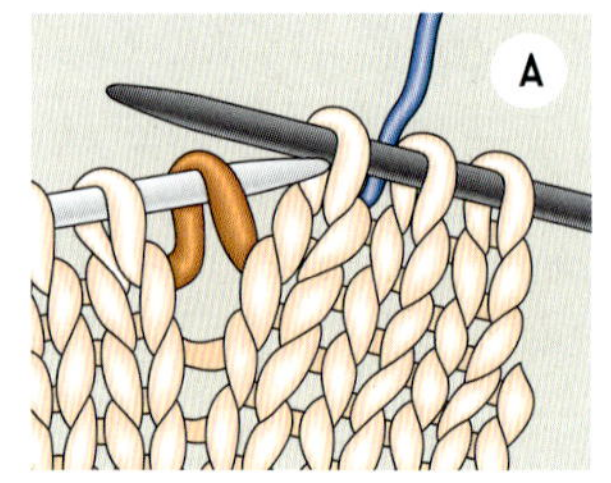

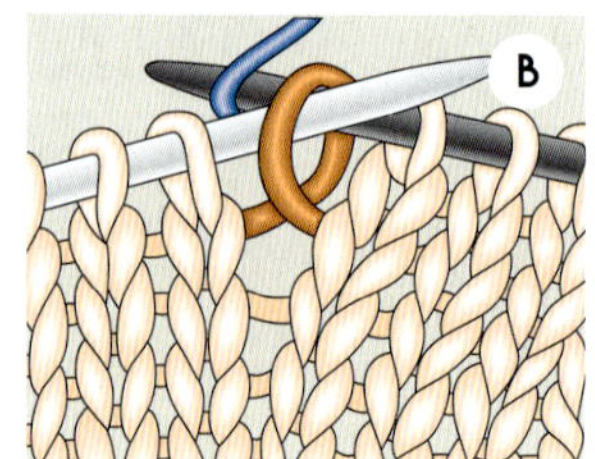

MAKE ONE RIGHT (M1R)

This technique creates a right-leaning 1-stitch knit increase.

1. Insert the left-hand needle from back to front into the bar between the stitches on each needle, and place it on the left-hand needle (C).

2. Knit into the front of the loop, creating an extra stitch (D).

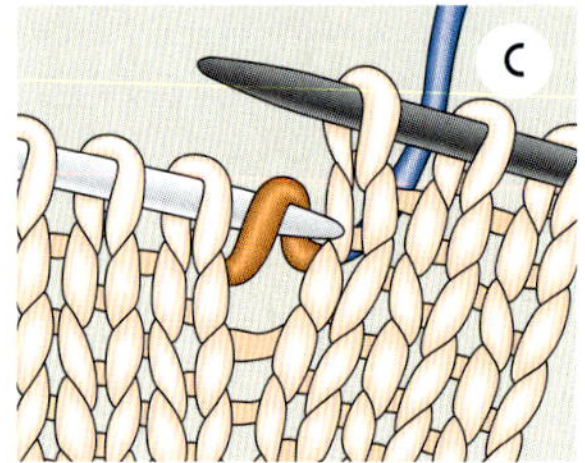

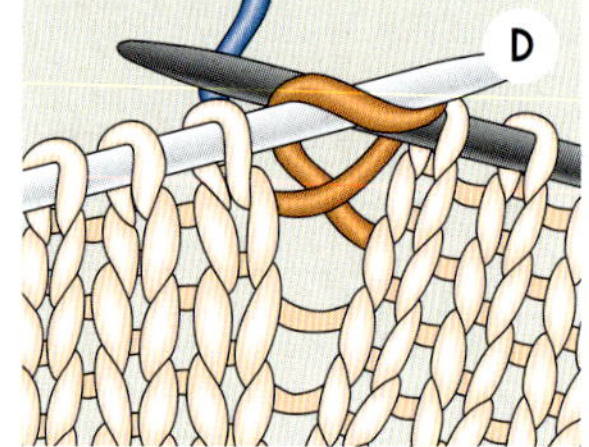

KNIT TWO TOGETHER (K2TOG)

This technique creates a right-leaning 1-stitch knit decrease.

Insert the tip of the right-hand needle into the front of the next two stitches, starting with the second stitch on the left-hand needle, and knit them together as 1 stitch.

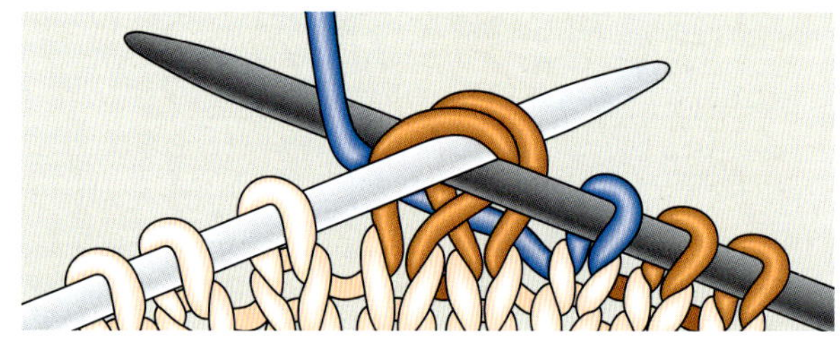

SLIP SLIP KNIT (SSK)

This technique creates a left-leaning 1-stitch knit decrease.

1. Slip the next 2 stitches onto the right-hand needle, as if to knit (E).

2. Knit them together as 1 stitch through the backs of the loops (F).

3. The finished decrease will lean to the left (G).

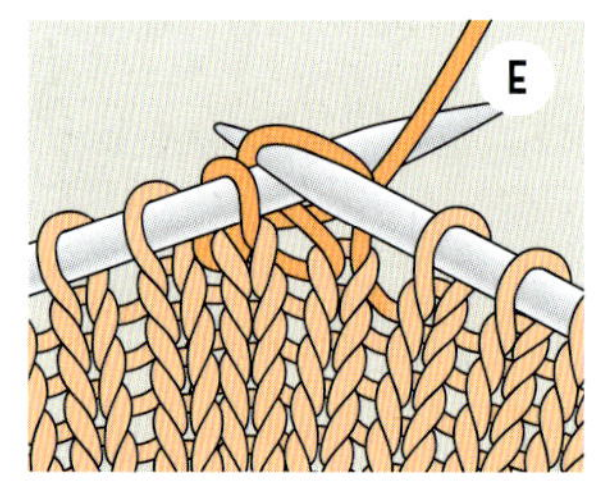

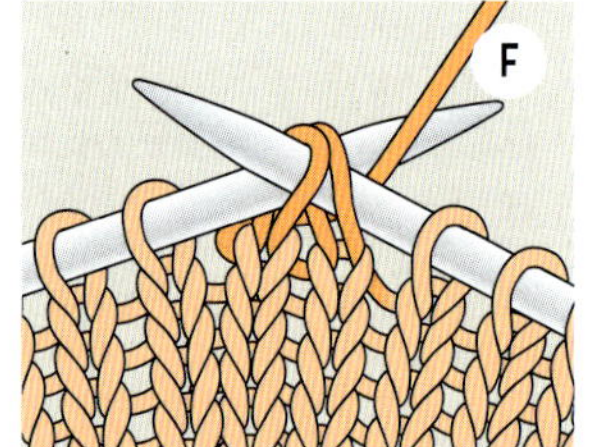

COLOURWORK

STRANDED COLOURWORK

When working with two yarn colours in a row, one colour will always be carried along the wrong side of the fabric until it is needed again.

1. Hold the colour you no longer need at the back and pick up the colour to work the next stitch (A).
2. Repeat to change back to the first colour again (B). Hold the colours in the same order each time – see Before You Begin: Colour Dominance.
3. On the wrong side, the unused colours should form neat strands on the back of the fabric (C). If you need to carry the yarn more than a few stitches, it's best to twist the two yarns together at intervals to hold the unused strand close to the wrong side of the fabric.

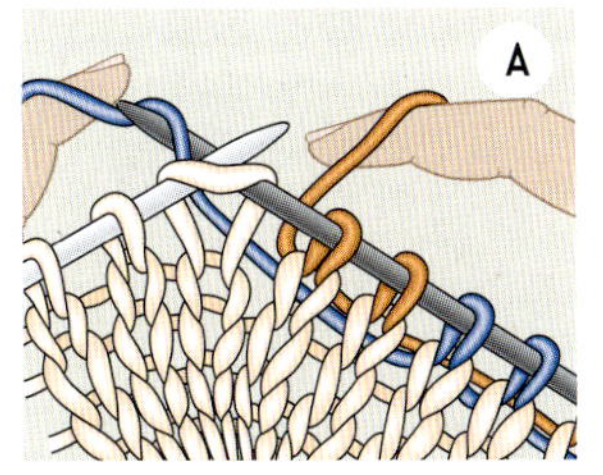

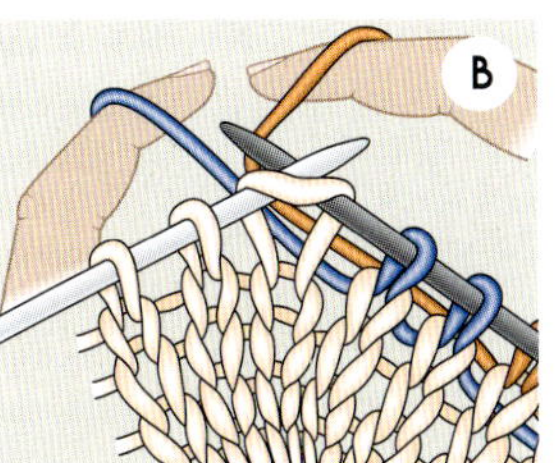

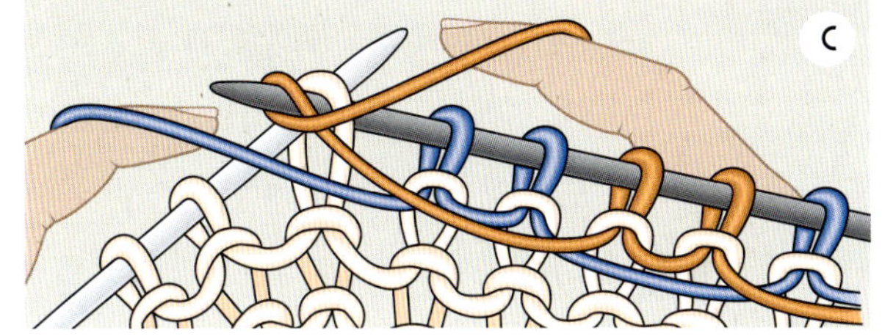

DUPLICATE STITCH

A method of adding coloured stitches over the top of existing knitted stitches in St St. Follow the chart for the colours to use and which stitches to work over.

1. Thread a length of yarn into a yarn needle and secure the yarn end at the back of the work. Bring the yarn through the right side of the fabric at the bottom of a stitch (D).
2. Insert the needle under both 'legs' of the stitch above and pull the yarn through (E).
3. Insert the needle back into the bottom of the first stitch to make the first duplicate stitch (F).
4. Bring the yarn out again at the bottom of the next stitch to be worked (G).

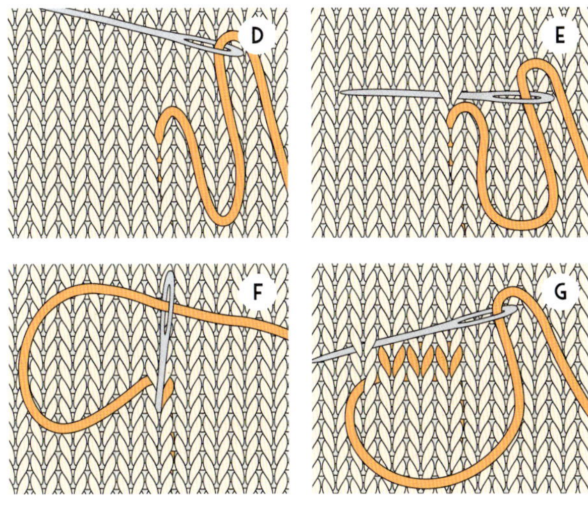

FINISHING TECHNIQUES

STRETCHY CAST-OFF (BIND-OFF)

The yarn overs made between the stitches create a very stretchy cast-off (bound-off) edge.

1. Knit the first stitch and then bring the yarn over the needle from back to front (A).
2. Knit the next stitch and then use the tip of the left-hand needle to lift the first stitch and the yarn over together over the second stitch and off the right-hand needle (B).
3. The first stitch has now been cast (bound) off (C).

Repeat these steps until you have cast (bound) off all the stitches.

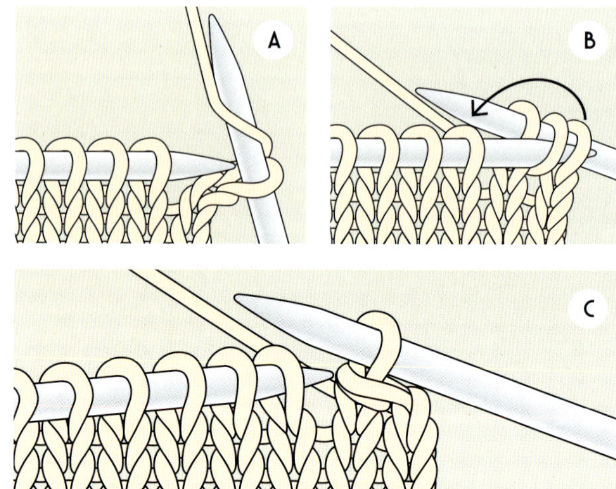

WHIP STITCH

This simple stitch is useful for sewing down folded necklines.

Fold the neckline over to the inside of the neck. Thread the yarn needle with a length of matching yarn and secure the end on the wrong side. Take the needle through one neckband edge stitch and then diagonally across through a stitch on the inside neck. Continue in this way to the end of the join.

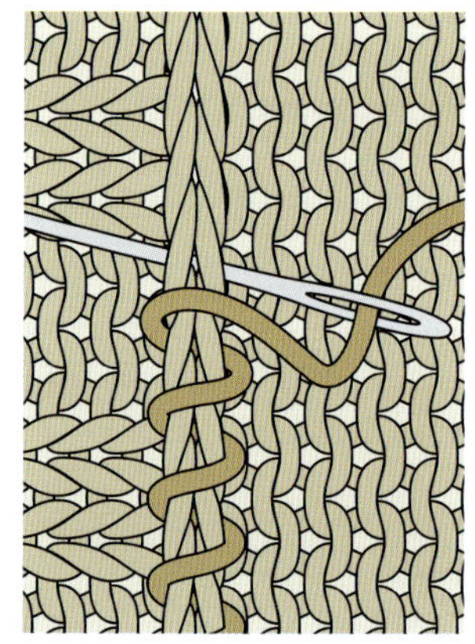

WEAVING IN ENDS

This is the last step in the project, to neaten up yarn ends on the wrong side of your work.

With the wrong side facing you, thread the yarn end into a yarn needle. Weave the yarn end through the back bumps of the stitches, working in the opposite direction to the knitted stitches. Try to weave ends into the same colour stitch and weave through at least 6–8 stitches. Trim the yarn end close to the work.

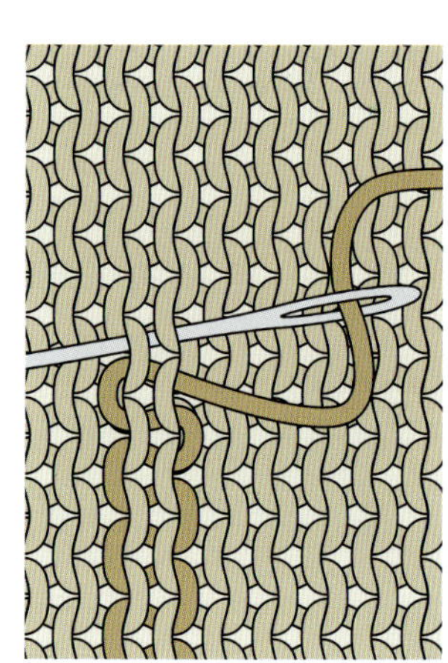

ABBREVIATIONS

CC	contrast colour
cm	centimetre
DPNs	double-pointed needles
DS	double stitch
g	gram
in	inch
k	knit
k2tog	knit 2 stitches together (decreases 1 stitch)
M1L	make 1 left (increases 1 stitch)
M1R	make 1 right (increases 1 stitch)
MC	main colour
mm	millimetre
oz	ounce
p	purl
sm	slip marker
ssk	slip slip knit (decreases 1 stitch)
st(s)	stitch(es)
St St	Stocking (stockinette) stitch

SUPPLIERS

Filcolana (Denmark)	www.filcolana.dk
Hillesvåg (Norway)	www.ull.no
Novita (Finland)	www.novitaknits.com
Rauma Garn (Norway)	www.raumagarn.no
Järbo (Sweden)	www.jarbo.se
Istex (Iceland)	www.istex.is
Färgkraft (Sweden):	www.fargkraft.com
SKeW Designs (Sweden)	www.skewdesign.se

ABOUT THE AUTHOR

Marita Clementz is a Swedish/Finnish knitwear designer. She lives in Sweden and is mother to twins. She loves to knit with natural fibres, creating big, bold patterns with a wide range of colours and yarns. Her philosophy is that colours bring joy to our lives, and her mission is to create as much joy as she can. When she is not knitting, she loves to spend time outdoors in her garden, hiking in the Scandinavian countryside, and travelling the world.

Instagram: **@maritaclementzyarnart**

Facebook: **Marita Clementz YarnArt**

Facebook group: **Sticka med Marita (Knit with Marita)**

ACKNOWLEDGMENTS

I want to thank my family for inspiring and supporting my creativity, and for looking so wonderful in all the sweaters. I would also like to thank my Instagram community – you have made it possible for me to write this book, and put these patterns out into the world. Lastly, thank you to the team at David & Charles, who have helped me to make this book a reality.

INDEX

A DAVID AND CHARLES BOOK

David and Charles is an imprint
of David and Charles, Ltd
Suite A, Tourism House, Pynes Hill, Exeter, EX2 5WS

First published in the UK and USA in 2025

A catalogue record for this book is available from the British Library.

ISBN-13: 9781446314395 paperback
ISBN-13: 9781446314401 EPUB

This book has been printed on paper from approved suppliers and made from pulp from sustainable sources.

Printed in China by Asia Pacific Offset for:
David and Charles, Ltd
Suite A, Tourism House, Pynes Hill, Exeter, EX2 5WS

10 9 8 7 6 5 4 3 2 1

Publishing Director: Ame Verso
Senior Commissioning Editor: Sarah Callard
Publishing Manager: Jeni Chown
Editor: Jessica Cropper
Project Editor: Rachael Prest
Head of Design: Sam Staddon
Designer: Lucy Ridley and Marieclare Mayne
Pre-press Designer: Susan Reansbury
Illustrations: Kuo Kang Chen
Photography: Maria Eberfors and Jason Jenkins
Production Manager: Beverley Richardson

David and Charles publishes high-quality books on a wide range of subjects. For more information visit www.davidandcharles.com.

Share your makes with us on social media using **#dandcbooks** and follow us on Facebook and Instagram by searching for **@dandcbooks.**

Layout of the digital edition of this book may vary depending on reader hardware and display settings.